# HEBREWS

# BRINGING THE BIBLE TO LIFE

*Genesis*, by John H. Walton, Janet Nygren, and Karen H. Jobes
(12 sessions)

*Esther*, by Karen H. Jobes and Janet Nygren
(8 sessions)

*John*, by Gary M. Burge, Karen Lee-Thorp, and Karen H. Jobes
(12 sessions)

*Romans*, by Douglas J. Moo, Karen Lee-Thorp, and Karen H. Jobes
(12 sessions)

*Ephesians*, by Klyne Snodgrass, Karen Lee-Thorp, and Karen H. Jobes
(6 sessions)

*Hebrews*, by George H. Guthrie, Janet Nygren, and Karen H. Jobes
(8 sessions)

BRINGING
THE
**BIBLE**
TO **LIFE**

# HEBREWS

## Running the Race Before Us

George H. Guthrie
Janet Nygren
*Series Editor, Karen H. Jobes*

**ZONDERVAN**.com/
AUTHOR**TRACKER**
*follow your favorite authors*

We want to hear from you. Please send your comments about this book to us in care of zreview@zondervan.com. Thank you.

**ZONDERVAN®**

*Bringing the Bible to Life: Hebrews*
Copyright © 2008 by George H. Guthrie, Janet Nygren, and Karen H. Jobes

ISBN 978-0-310-27653-1

*Interior design by Michelle Espinoza*

*Printed in the United States of America*

08 09 10 11 12 13 14 • 23 22 21 20 19 18 17 16 15 14 13 12 11 10 9 8 7 6 5 4 3 2 1

# CONTENTS

# SERIES PREFACE

Have you ever been in a small-group Bible study where the leader read a passage from the Bible and then invited the members of the group to share what the passage meant to them? God wants to speak to each person individually through the Bible, but such an approach to group study can often be a frustrating and shallow experience for both leader and participants. And while the same passage can speak in various ways into people's lives, the meat of the Word is found in what the biblical writer intended to say about God and our relationship to him. The Bringing the Bible to Life series is for those who are ready to move from a surface reading of the Bible into a deeper understanding of God's Word.

But the Bible, though perhaps familiar, was written in ancient languages and in times quite different from our own, so most readers need a bit more help getting to a deeper understanding of its message. A study that begins and ends with what a passage "means to me" leaves the meaning of the passage unanchored and adrift in the thoughts—and perhaps the misunderstanding—of the reader. But who has time to delve into the history, language, cultures, and theology of the Bible? That's the work of biblical scholars who spend their lives researching, teaching, and writing about the ancient Scriptures. The need is to get the fruit of all that research into the hands of those in small-group Bible studies.

Zondervan's NIV Application Commentary (NIVAC) series was written to bring the best of evangelical biblical scholarship to those who want to know *both* the historical meaning of the biblical text *and* its contemporary significance. This companion series, Bringing the Bible to Life, is intended to bring that material into small-group studies in an easy-to-use format. Pastors, Christian education teachers, and small-group leaders whether in church, campus, or home settings will find these guides to be an enriching resource.

Each guide in the series provides an introduction to the biblical book that concisely summarizes the background information needed to better understand the original historical context. Six to twelve sessions per guide, with each session consisting of eleven or twelve discussion questions, allow a focused study that moves beyond superficial Bible reading. Relevant excerpts from the corresponding NIVAC commentary provide easy access into additional material for those interested in going even deeper. A closing section in each session assists the group in responding to God's word together or individually. Guidance for leading each session is included, making the task of small-group leadership more manageable for busy lives.

If you want to move from the biblical text to contemporary life on solid ground, this series has been written for you.

Karen H. Jobes, PhD
Gerald F. Hawthorne Professor of
New Testament Greek and Exegesis
Wheaton College and Graduate School

# AUTHOR'S PREFACE

D r. William Lane, my friend and mentor on Hebrews, who has now gone to be with the Lord, once wrote, "Hebrews is a delight for the person who enjoys puzzles." If you have ever struggled with the topical twists and turns of this sometimes difficult book, or asked about its authorship, or mulled over Melchizedek, or racked your brain over the modern relevance of its seemingly obscure Old Testament practices, I am sure you will agree. Yet, I am convinced that Hebrews has so much to offer any of us who want to follow Jesus faithfully in the modern world and so much to say to the church as a whole about the kind of community life that fosters endurance in the faith.

That is why, when Zondervan asked me to write the *NIV Application Commentary: Hebrews* (published in 1998), I was thrilled with the opportunity. My hope was that the commentary might help communities of believers think more clearly about this wonderful book and, therefore, live more effectively for Christ.

The author of this study guide, Janet Nygren, has done a great job in creating what we hope will be a helpful tool for both individuals and groups, guiding you with probing questions as you work your way through Hebrews and the commentary. My prayer is that you will study hard, reflect deeply, and live out the truths that you find here—and that, above all, you will see Jesus more clearly, know him more intimately, and grasp the significance of what he, our great High Priest, has accomplished on our behalf. May the Lord bless you as you study.

George H. Guthrie

# INTRODUCTION[1]

A brand new Christian starts going to church and wonders about other people who don't seem very excited to be there. A friendly face at a party says she gave up on churches long ago and does faith her own way. A missionary prays for a devoted follower of Christ who isn't sure he can take the heat from his family about his faith. A pastor sadly reflects on the people he no longer sees in worship. A Sunday school teacher debates whether or not to teach next year—surely it's someone else's turn. A high school student wonders why he's not getting more out of worship. Some Christians are weary and need encouragement. Others face intense pressure to walk away from faith in Jesus Christ. Still others are in a spiritual lethargy, just going through the motions while their minds are on other, more pressing issues. And then there are those that you are shocked to hear call themselves Christians at all.

The book of Hebrews takes all these people head on. Pay Attention! Hang On! Be Careful! Keep Going! What you think and what you do have eternal consequences, and it matters "Today." The author presents his readers with a vivid picture of Christ—who he is, what he did, how he relates to us—and how Jesus single-handedly restores us so that we can stand before God himself. The author challenges his readers to make their faith sure by persevering to the end. He encourages his readers to love one another and cheer others on when they are wavering. In an environment that puts pressures on the Christian faith, the message of Hebrews is as critical today as it was when it was first read to a congregation centuries ago.

## ORIGINAL SETTING

No one knows who wrote this sermon-like letter, and our understanding of the setting and timing is pretty shaky as well. But it's clear from the letter itself that the original audience needed encouragement. They certainly knew something about Christianity and had demonstrated their faith in action under pressure in the past. But at least some of them seemed to be drifting away over time. Add to the mix some persecution and peer pressure to go back to old ways, and there was good reason for the author to address the group. Educated guessing suggests the letter was written in the mid–60s AD near Rome, where there was a significant Jewish population that had converted to Christianity. That would explain the frequent quotes from the Old Testament and familiarity with Jewish thinking, as well as a temptation to slide back to Jewish customs, and pressure or persecution from different groups in the community.

I've noticed while working on Hebrews that I hear it quoted quite a lot — either specific verses that are in common Christian usage, or thinking that seems to come straight from the pages of the book. Why is that? Maybe I just have an extra-sensitive antenna for Hebrews material right now, but I believe it has more to do with how central the message of Hebrews is to thinking and living out the Christian faith. The author is keen to establish a strong foundation for understanding and interpreting God's Word properly, but he is equally insistent about putting thoughts into actions so people really grow in their faith.

Whether you are studying Hebrews on your own, or looking at it together with a small group, I hope you will find it to be both an encouragement and challenge to your faith. Take time to pray, think, listen, and respond. Investing this time in growing in your faith has implications for you and for those around you, today and for eternity.

## NOTE

1. This introduction is based on *The NIV Application Commentary: Hebrews* (hereafter referred to as *NIVAC: Hebrews*) by George H. Guthrie (Grand Rapids, Mich.: Zondervan, 1998), 17–38.

# PAY ATTENTION: JESUS IS GREAT!

## Hebrews 1:1–2:4

How has God spoken to you? Has he spoken through a favorite verse or book? The touch of a friend? The brilliant shades of a sunset? A stirring sermon? By your ability to persevere through tough circumstances when you know it wasn't your own strength? Is life different now than it used to be? The author of Hebrews wants to appeal to his audience in a way that truly speaks to them. He starts with what is familiar, drawing on old Jewish concepts that are almost second nature to his original audience, but also wants to challenge them with fresh insights. When things are tough, as they were for the readers of Hebrews, sometimes it helps to see things from a new perspective to understand how they are still relevant to our lives. God's solution to our problems was radical, but we — as well as the original audience — can lose sight of that. Listen to the author of Hebrews and refresh your perspective on who Jesus is — God's very own Son.

## A NEW REVELATION[1]

*Read Hebrews 1:1–4.*

Chances are, if you ask an American about African-American history, they'll mention something about slavery, the Civil War, Abraham Lincoln, and civil rights. A European would no doubt have some inkling of the wars and monarchies of his or her own country. In the same way, there is a lot of Jewish history that would be second nature to the readers of the epistle to the Hebrews. You don't have to be an expert to get the gist of it, but a little understanding will make this book a lot richer.

*"In the past God spoke to our ancestors through the prophets at many times and in various ways, but in these last days he has spoken to us by his Son"* *(Heb. 1:1 – 2).*

1. Take a minute to think about some of the various ways God spoke through Hebrew prophets in the Old Testament. The following list is a sampling to get you thinking if you are unfamiliar with their stories.

Noah (Gen. 6:9 – 22)

Abraham (Gen. 15:1 – 6)

Jacob (Gen. 28:10 – 22)

Moses (Ex. 3:1 – 10; 19:16 – 20:18)

Nathan (2 Sam. 12:1 – 10)

Jeremiah (Jer. 18:1 – 10; 24:3 – 10)

Hosea (Hos. 1:2 – 3)

Jonah (Jonah 1:1 – 3, 17; 4:5 – 8)

How was God's revelation in the Old Testament different from how he spoke through Christ?

2. The first four verses of Hebrews give us an excellent summary of the author's beliefs. What can you learn about Jesus' relationship to God the Father (Heb. 1:2)? His responsibilities concerning creation (vv. 2–3)? His similarity to God the Father (v. 3)? His accomplishments (v. 3)? His status (v. 4)? How do these things "speak to us" about God?

**GOING DEEPER**

Both ancient Jewish homiletics and Greco-Roman oratory placed great emphasis on a work having an appropriate beginning.... In that introduction the speaker presented the main topic(s) or text of his speech or sermon and sought to rivet the attention of the audience. Our author accomplishes both with admirable skill.[2]

3. Based on this introduction, what major themes would you expect to see in Hebrews?

The author of Hebrews is not just a great theologian who weaves together great themes and connects Old Testament ideas with Jesus' work on earth. He also has a pastor's heart that is very much concerned with the day-to-day life of the people he's writing to. Throughout the book we'll see him going back and forth between these two roles. But with this in mind, let's take one more look at these beginning verses before moving on.

4. Because Jesus has spoken to us "in these last days," what difference can it make in the nitty-gritty details of daily life? Take, for example, the fact that he provided purification for sins (Heb. 1:3). It sounds very theological, but how might it affect what you say the day after you have a huge argument with someone you love? Try doing this with two or three of the characteristics you came up with in question 2.

## JESUS EXALTED[3]

*Read Hebrews 1:5–14.*

It's a little intimidating for the average reader today to wade through so many quotes in the very first chapter of Hebrews. But at the time it was written such chains of quotations served an author's purpose:

**GOING DEEPER**

During the era in which Hebrews was written, teachers of Scripture … built support for a theological position by stringing together various Old Testament texts. Such "chain quotations" offered defense of the position being taught through the quantity of support given.… The desired effect was to offer so much evidence that your listeners shook their heads in agreement with you by the end of these quotations.[4]

5. When the author uses scriptural quotes like this to support his argument, what assumptions can we say he is making about Scripture? Do you hold the same assumptions about Scripture?

It's helpful to read the Scripture quotations as three pairs. The first two quotes are about the unique relationship of God the Father and his Son. They sound almost the same in the quotation, but the contexts are quite different in the Old Testament sources.

*Read Psalm 2:1–7.*

6.  What does this psalm say about the relationship between God and his Son? What's God's attitude toward anyone who might try to plot against him or his Son?

*Read 2 Samuel 7:11b–13.*

*"I will establish the throne of his kingdom forever" (2 Sam. 7:13).*

7.  Nathan's prophecy to David about building a house for God was fulfilled in his era by David's son Solomon, but for the author of Hebrews to quote it about Jesus points to God's plan for a much greater and longer-lasting kingdom. What does this say about the time frame for God's plans? How do God's plans for Jesus contrast to those for the angels (Heb. 1:5a)?

The second set of quotes (Heb. 1:6–7) presents the role of angels as inferior to the role of the Son.

**GOING DEEPER**

[The term firstborn] ... continues the idea of sonship established thus far in Hebrews.... A firstborn son had a special place in the heart of his father ... shared the father's authority, and inherited the lion's share of his property.[5]

8. According to the second pair of quotations (Heb. 1:6–7; see also v. 14), what role do angels play in God's kingdom?

The third pair of quotations (Heb. 1:8–12) focuses again on the superior position of the Son.

*Read Psalm 45:1–7.*

9. This psalm is described in the TNIV Study Bible as "a song in praise to the king on his wedding day." What characterizes this king and his kingdom? Is he a king you would want to be ruled by?

*Read Psalm 102:1–12, 25–27.*

10. Psalm 102 is described as the prayer of an afflicted man. What do you learn about the eternal nature of Jesus in this psalm, particularly in contrast to humankind?

**GOING DEEPER**

Hebrews 1:5–14 climaxes with the quotation of Psalm 110:1, which presents clearly the exaltation of Christ to the right hand of God. This Old Testament text further demonstrates that the preacher's [author's] main interest at this point lies in impressing on the listeners the supreme position and authority of the Son.[6]

## PAY ATTENTION![7]

*Read Hebrews 2:1–4.*

Throughout Hebrews, the author switches back and forth between exposition and exhortation[8] — reminding his audience of God's truth, then emphasizing what they should actually do about it. You may have heard the phrase "What's the 'therefore' there for?" Well, Hebrews is a great place to ask that question. In this section, we come to the first exhortation, the author's reason for emphasizing everything we've studied so far about the exaltation of Christ.

11. If you lived during a time of persecution and change, as was likely for the original audience, why would it be important to hear the author's challenge in 2:1–4? Would what you've heard so far be a comfort or a challenge (or both)? Why?

12. In light of 1:1–2 and 2:2–4, how do you think God expects us to respond to his Word as revealed through Christ?

## RESPONDING TO GOD'S WORD

### *IN YOUR GROUP:*

I can remember a discussion I had once, in which a couple of people were excitedly sharing how their "guardian angels" had saved them from some disaster. Of course I was thankful for their safety, and can relate to experiences myself where some mysterious hand of protection was surely at work, but I remember leaving somewhat ill at ease. It seemed like something was missing from that conversation, though I couldn't quite put my finger on it. The next morning at church, we sang "Fairest Lord Jesus," and it all straightened out in my mind. Angels are wonderful servants of God, but if we end up worshiping them we can miss out on the greater glories of God himself.

Read through or sing together this wonderful hymn originally written by German Jesuits in the seventeenth century and translated by Joseph A. Seiss.[9] Think about how it reflects what we have learned in Hebrews 1, and use it to worship our beautiful Savior with your whole heart.

*Fairest Lord Jesus, Ruler of all nature,*
*O Thou of God and man the Son,*
*Thee will I cherish, Thee will I honor,*
*Thou, my soul's glory, joy, and crown.*

*Fair are the meadows, fairer still the woodlands.*
*Robed in the blooming garb of spring;*
*Jesus is fairer, Jesus is purer,*
*Who makes the woeful heart to sing.*

*Fair is the sunshine, fairer still the moonlight,*
*And all the twinkling starry host;*
*Jesus shines brighter, Jesus shines purer*
*Than all the angels heaven can boast.*

*Beautiful Savior! Lord of all the nations!*
*Son of God and Son of Man!*
*Glory and honor, praise, adoration,*
*Now and forever more be Thine.*

## ON YOUR OWN:

How has God spoken to you? Think about experiences in which you felt that you got to know God better. Write a personal letter to Jesus telling him about them, and expressing your appreciation for those times.

## NOTES

1. This section is based on *NIVAC: Hebrews*, 45–65.
2. Guthrie, 52.
3. This section is based on *NIVAC: Hebrews*, 66–82.
4. Guthrie, 67.
5. Guthrie, 69.
6. Guthrie, 77.
7. This section is based on *NIVAC: Hebrews*, 83–95.
8. See Guthrie, 27–30.
9. *http://www.cyberhymnal.org/htm/f/a/l/faljesus.htm* (March 14, 2008).

# HANG ON: JESUS IS ONE OF US!

## Hebrews 2:5–3:6

Hot or cold. Up or down. Naughty or nice. Success or failure. We often think in extremes that are mutually exclusive. Yet the author of Hebrews introduces extreme opposites that work exclusively to our advantage: Jesus, the exalted one, is humbled. Who would have thought that God would come up with such a plan? What genius! It breaks all the other religious molds, and provides a great source of courage and hope for us to hang on to in the midst of rough times.

## JESUS HUMBLED[1]

*Read Hebrews 2:5–9.*

1. In the first session we firmly established how great Jesus is compared to the angels, giving us every reason to pay attention to what his life and words say to us. How does 2:5 relate to the author's argument from chapter 1?

2. Hebrews 2:6–8a sets up a contrast to chapter 1 by quoting Psalm 8:4–6. In case you don't quite get his point from the psalm, the author gives his own interpretation in Hebrews 2:8b–9. How is Jesus depicted differently here compared to chapter 1? What's the author's explanation for this switch?

**GOING DEEPER**

The statement about the Incarnation in Psalm 8, as interpreted by our author, reads, "You made him a little lower than the angels [heavenly beings]." ... [T]his phrase can be understood in two ways: a small measure of distance or substance ("just a little lower"), or a small amount of time ("for a little while"). This latter meaning seems to fit the context better since the author is not interested in the degree to which the Son was of a lower status than the angels. Moreover, the author is expressing the thought that Christ walked the earth as a human being for a brief time before being exalted back to heaven.[2]

3. In 2:8 we are told that "God left nothing that is not subject to him" (NIV). In other words, Jesus rules—there is not a speck in the universe that is not under his control. But wait! His next sentence says, "Yet at present we do not see everything subject to him" (NIV). Is this a contradiction? Would his statement be comforting or confusing to his readers? How about to you?

## JESUS AS A BROTHER[3]

*Read Hebrews 2:10–18.*

Sometimes we can begin to take Jesus' humiliation for granted. We've heard so often that Jesus came to earth that it just seems natural for him to do so. But keep in mind why he was exalted in chapter 1—the precious Son of God was anointed with oil because he was beloved and set apart. There was no one else worthy of inheriting God's kingdom. Lowering himself for a little while and subjecting himself to the abuse of all the forces of evil was a very big deal.

4. Sprinkled throughout 2:10–18, we get glimpses of Jesus' purpose for coming to earth. What phrases in this section point to what Jesus accomplished? How do these things affect your regard for Jesus?

5. Jesus had to be equipped, in a sense, in order to accomplish his purpose. This is not to say that he wasn't already perfect, holy, and sinless. But there are certain experiences humans go through that God never went through until he himself became human. What phrases in 2:10 – 18 describe the unique ways Jesus was equipped for his "job" on earth?

As we've seen before, the author of Hebrews uses Old Testament Scripture to support his points. The quotes in Hebrews 2:12 – 13 (from Ps. 22:22 and Isa. 8:17b – 18) were both familiar to the early church and understood as messianic, that is, prophesying what the Christ would be like.[4] Psalm 22 should even sound familiar to most modern Christian audiences, since much of it foreshadows Jesus' words and experience of suffering on the cross.

6. How do the quotes in 2:12 – 13 put Jesus on the same level as us? What does it mean to you to be called a "brother" of Christ?

**GOING DEEPER**

In ancient culture the image of brotherhood spoke of the intimacy of relationship, shared experience, and loyalty. Thus, the image communicates a close association, such as in a fraternal relationship. Hebrews 2:12 does not mean Jesus only proclaims God's name to males, but as the parallel in the next line suggests, he announces God's name to all those in "the congregation," that is, the people of God with whom he enjoys an intimate relationship.[5]

7. Have you ever wished there was someone else who could relate to how you feel about something? Do you know what it's like to comfort or be comforted because of having shared a similar experience with someone? Think of some examples in your own life.

How does the humanity of Jesus make him more approachable? How can you take greater advantage of this aspect of who Jesus is?

8. How is God's plan for saving us, as described in Scripture and particularly in these verses, different from other belief systems?

We need someone greater than ourselves to come into our experience from the outside and lead us, teach us, and rescue us. In short, we need a champion to storm the gates of our prisons and liberate us, ripping the keys to enslavement from the devil's grip and setting our feet on the path of true life.

What is surprising is the form our champion took and the means of our liberation. The one of all power took the position of the powerless. The Lord of life drank deeply of death. The way he brought us up to God was by coming completely down to, even below our level, taking the form of a servant. Since we could not save ourselves, he did not save himself from the worst of human experiences. The limitless Lord of the universe took on limitations in order to free us from ours, and nowhere are our limitations more clearly recognized than in face of death.[6]

# JESUS, WORTHY OF FOLLOWING[7]

*Read Hebrews 3:1–6.*

9. Jesus may have lowered himself for a little while to relate to our level, but look what's happened to us! How has our name and calling changed according to 3:1, as a result of being included in the same family as Jesus?

10. In light of what we've learned about Jesus in this session, what would it mean for you to "fix your thoughts on Jesus" on a daily basis?

For Jews, Moses had always been the extreme example of what it meant to be a great servant of God. In fact, some sources suggest that he was regarded with higher status even than angels, whom we've already seen to be highly regarded at that time.[8] In case there's any doubt in the minds of the audience, the author of Hebrews makes it clear in 3:2–6 that Jesus in his exalted state is not only superior to angels, but also superior to Moses as the humble servant.

11. According to 3:3–6, why is Jesus a better example of a servant to follow than Moses?

**GOING DEEPER** Since believers are "children," we especially need an example of someone who has lived out a filial faithfulness. Thus Jesus, as the Son of God, provides an example superior to that of even the greatest of Old Testament figures. Furthermore, as the Creator he has a greater inherent authority than Moses, who was a part of his creation. Thus, the author builds on the greatness of Moses and asserts that as great as this religious figure might be, Jesus must be the object of a Christian's ultimate focus.[9]

12. How would following in the footsteps of a beloved family member be different from following the example of a hero from history?

## RESPONDING TO GOD'S WORD

*IN YOUR GROUP:*

Discuss specific heroes you have looked up to. What qualities did you appreciate about him or her? Are there things about your hero that you wish you didn't know? How would following Jesus as your hero change the way you do things?

## ON YOUR OWN:[10]

Skim through the gospel of Luke this week, slowing down to focus on one-on-one interactions of Jesus with different individuals. How do these moments emphasize Jesus' ability to relate to us and address our concerns in a personal way?

## NOTES

1. This section is based on *NIVAC: Hebrews*, 96–105.
2. Guthrie, 98.
3. This section is based on *NIVAC: Hebrews*, 106–123.
4. Guthrie, 109.
5. Guthrie, 114.
6. Guthrie, 119–120.
7. This section is based on *NIVAC: Hebrews*, 124–128, 131–133.
8. Guthrie, 127.
9. Guthrie, 133.
10. My thanks to Jayne Clarke, who uses this idea in her biblical counseling.

# BE CAREFUL TO LEARN FROM THE PAST

## Hebrews 3:7 – 4:13; 12:18 – 29

Does history repeat itself? A Christian worldview could be described more as an unfolding story than a circle-of-life sort of philosophy. But that's not to say that we don't repeat mistakes! A student of history might propose that every imaginable mistake has already been made numerous times in history — they just get dressed up a bit differently each time they're made. The author of Hebrews would love for the people who read his words to learn from mistakes in the past to spare them some serious trouble — and that goes for us as well as his original readers!

## THE DESERT WANDERERS[1]

*Read Hebrews 3:7 – 19.*

The author sets the tone in this section with a quote from Psalm 95:7–8, "Today, if only you would hear his voice, do not harden your hearts." These verses are quoted three times (Heb. 3:7–8, 15; 4:7), tying the section together with quite a firm warning.

1. The author of Hebrews takes a little liberty with the verses he's quoting in order to make his point. What constitutes "the rebellion" that he talks about in 3:8 and 3:15, according to Psalm 95:8? What other events from the period of desert wanderings might he be thinking of (e.g., Ex. 15:22–17:7; 32:1–10; Num. 11:1–3; 12:1–14:45; 20:1–13)? Do you think the author of Hebrews is justified in using the term "rebellion"?

2. From your brief survey of the Old Testament passages in the last question, do you think God was being overly harsh with the Israelites? What evidence did they have that God was working in their behalf? What indications did they have in their recent past of how God deals with hardened hearts (Ex. 7–14)? What were the consequences for their desert rebellion (Heb. 3:16–19)?

3. This little history lesson doesn't come in a vacuum. What is the author of Hebrews warning his readers against (3:12–15)? By implication, what could the consequences be? What is his antidote?

4. Is the warning equally valid today? Keep in mind that the author is addressing "brothers and sisters, who share in the heavenly calling" (3:1, 12). What dangers does a Christian today face in regard to "a sinful, unbelieving heart that turns away from the living God" (3:12)?

**GOING DEEPER**

For the author of Hebrews, those drifting away from God with hearts callused by sin are in serious trouble.... Hebrews 3:6, 14 suggest that assurance of salvation—assurance that we have partaken of the grace of God—in part depends on the vitality of one's ongoing relationship with Christ and the church. This is not to suggest that one earns salvation through faithfulness but that faithfulness is evidence of one's salvation. It may be that a "drifter" truly has a relationship with Christ and will come around again to Christian commitment. Yet, the drifter in a state of drifting has no assurance of his or her right standing before God since God's grace is not being manifested in that person's life.[2]

# THE PROMISED REST[3]

*Read Hebrews 4:1 – 13.*

The TNIV and NIV rendering of "be careful" (4:1) is a bit tame — "let us fear" would be more appropriate.[4] Don't take this warning too lightly! It's addressed to all believers! There was a whole generation of people who certainly looked like believers on the surface but *they did not enter the promised rest*. It's so easy to think of others who qualify as having hard hearts, but the author is pointing his finger at you: "Today, if *you* hear his voice, do not harden your hearts."

5. Do you consider yourself to be someone who hears God's voice? Using 4:12 – 13 as an examination tool, how does your heart look under the bright light and sharp scalpel of God's Word? If you're not entirely sure, ask someone you live with!

Unfortunately, grumbling, disobedience, rebellion, and sin are still part of our attitudes toward God — we're a lot like the desert wanderers. So we've got to look beyond our own efforts of self-improvement to find hope. When we are called to turn *away* from something, it's always helpful to have an idea of what we're supposed to turn *toward* instead. God is quite consistent in showing us what is better, and he does it here with an understanding of what true "rest" should look like.

6. Even though the desert wanderers lived many centuries before Jesus Christ, 4:2 states that they had heard the good news of God's grace preached to them, just as we have, but it had no value to them because they did not combine it with faith. According to Leviticus 16:29–31, what did the Sabbath rest on the Day of Atonement consist of? How is this similar to the gospel preached to us?

7. Our rest is compared to the rest that God experienced on the seventh day of creation, when he rested from his work (4:9–10). In what way should we not work on the Sabbath? Is this rest that is spoken of here something we experience now or something waiting for us in the future?

**GOING DEEPER**

True rest, which involves ceasing from one's own work as God did at creation and entering God's promised blessing of forgiveness, cannot be had by slaves or desert wanderers. Rather, true rest is found in rightly relating to God through faith and obedience to his Word. Only by joining him in his creation rest and humbling ourselves in light of [Christ's] Day of Atonement sacrifice can we experience the Sabbath celebration reserved for God's people.[5]

8. Have you ever wondered, while preparing for a vacation, if all the effort involved will be worth it? Planning, making reservations, shopping, packing, arranging for the care of things at home while you're away, thinking through every last detail. On the surface, we might think entering rest should be effortless, but 4:11 urges us to "make every effort to enter that rest, so that no one will perish by following [the desert wanderers'] example of disobedience." What kind of effort is necessary for entering God's rest?

## TRUE WORSHIP[6]

*Read Hebrews 12:18 – 29.*

The author of Hebrews does not have a linear approach to the outline of his letter, moving on from one theme after he's exhausted the subject. Instead, he touches on themes and comes back to them again, as if he's thinking out loud, taking some side trips, then coming back to the original thought again. So while we're on the subject of desert wanderers, we're going to jump ahead temporarily to chapter 12 where we get another comparison between then and now.

9. When Hebrews was written, one principle used in preaching was *an argument from lesser to greater.* If something was true in a lesser situation, it would apply all the more in a more important situation.[7] Hebrews 12:25 – 27 uses this principle. Discuss the consequences of disobedience for the desert wanderers in chapters 3 – 4 in comparison with what could happen to us if we are disobedient. Why is it important to listen to God's warnings?

10. We've certainly seen that the consequences for disobedience are not something to be taken lightly. But we don't want to give the impression that faith is just built on fear, or doom and gloom. How has the believer's relationship with God changed from the time of the desert wanderers, as described in 12:18–21, compared to the present, as God has unfolded his plan of redemption, and most especially in light of of Jesus' work, as described in 12:22–24?

*"He is no fool who gives what he cannot keep to gain what he cannot lose."*
Jim Elliot

11. Remember that the warnings in Hebrews 3–4 were based on a quote from Psalm 95:7–8. Read the context of those verses in Psalm 95:1–7. Even though the author does not quote the beginning of the psalm, he may have had them in mind as he quotes the warnings. How does the first half of Psalm 95 as well as Hebrews 12:28–29 point to the response God desires from us? How does this provide balance to the warnings we've been looking at?

12. How would you characterize your worship, both personally and in your church? Does it reflect the fear of God that occurred at Mount Sinai for the desert wanderers, or does it capture the joy described at Mount Zion?

**GOING DEEPER**

If our lives reflect the gloom of Sinai more than the excitement of Zion, we do the kingdom poor publicity. This does not mean, of course, that we always are thrilled with our situations; but are we *characterized* by joy? That is a key question. If we are not, then the reality of Zion is not invading our lives. Perhaps we need a clearer view of that mountain and must hear again the song of the angels and the message of the sprinkled blood.[8]

## RESPONDING TO GOD'S WORD

*IN YOUR GROUP:*

Read Psalm 95 together aloud.

After vv. 1–2, pause to pray, focusing on praise and thanksgiving.

After vv. 3–5, pause to pray, focusing on God's creation and sovereignty.

After vv. 6–7, pause to pray, focusing on his care.

After vv. 8–11, pause to pray, asking for forgiveness for disobedience and hardened hearts.

*ON YOUR OWN:*

How much of your week could be characterized by rebellion? Keep a journal this week listing anything that qualifies as grumbling, disobedience, rebellion, or sin. How does it add up? At the end of the week (or each day), confess these faults to God, and thank him for the grace of forgiveness. Turn over a new leaf and start again for a new day or week!

## NOTES

1. This section is based on *NIVAC: Hebrews*, 129–147.
2. Guthrie, 142–143.
3. This section is based on *NIVAC: Hebrews*, 148–172.
4. Guthrie, 150.
5. Guthrie, 167.
6. This section is based on *NIVAC: Hebrews*, 416–432.
7. Guthrie, 25.
8. Guthrie, 430.

# DRAW NEAR BECAUSE WE HAVE A BETTER PRIEST

## Hebrews 4:14 – 5:10; 7:1 – 8:2

I was on a roller coaster ride recently that left me feeling rather wobbly by the time it finished. Never was the strong, young hand of the attendant at the end so welcome! I'm not sure I could have hoisted myself back up out of the car without his help. Having been reminded in the last session just how "wobbly" we can be when we really examine our hearts, even at the best of times, it is great news to know that there's someone, Jesus himself, who can sympathize with our "rough ride" and reach down to pull us back up out of our troubles and weaknesses.

### THE ROLE OF THE PRIEST[1]

*Read Hebrews 5:1 – 10.*

Maybe it's just me, but when I hear the term "priest," I think formal religion, rites, robes, unapproachable holiness—whether we're talking about pagan priests, Old Testament priests, Christian priests, or whatever—I don't think of warm fuzzies. The author of Hebrews uses this section to clarify what a priest did in his day, and begins to describe Jesus' qualifications for the job.

1.  According to 5:1–2, what is the essential purpose of the high priest?

*to offer gifts + sacrifices for sin*
*to have compassion on the ignorant*

2.  The job of high priest didn't originate just to keep someone busy. Why was it necessary in the first place to have a priest (see Gen. 3:8–10; Ex. 3:4–6)?

*to speak for the people*

What does the fact that God appointed a priest tell you about God (see Ex. 3:16–17, 4:29–31)?

*That god cared about the people + that he wanted the people to hear his word*

3. The role of high priest was a pretty select job. What criteria had to be met in order for a person to qualify as high priest, according to Hebrews 5:1–4? How did Jesus qualify (2:17–18; 5:5–10)?

*He was called of god*
*He offered gifts + sacrifice for the sins of people*
*He was son of god*
*He learned obedience by things he suffered*
*He had been tempted*

**GOING DEEPER**

As he introduces the book's great central section on Jesus' superior priesthood and offering (5:1–10:18), the author must begin by establishing the authority of Christ in a different vein, redirecting the argument toward the concept of Jesus' position and sacrifice as means of true relationship to God.... All that he will say about the high priesthood of Christ in the coming chapters flows from divine mandate. This is not just wrangling about obscure theological concepts. Rather, what the author wishes to say about Christ's appointment to the position of high priest derives from the heart of God, a fact witnessed to by the authority of God's decree.[2]

# WHO IS MELCHIZEDEK, ANYWAY?[3]

*Read Hebrews 7:1–10.*

*"Melchizedek king of Salem brought out bread and wine. He was priest of God Most High" (Gen. 14:18).*

No one knows very much about Melchizedek, the mysterious priest of God Most High and king of Salem, who is referred to elsewhere in Scripture only in Genesis 14:17–20 and Psalm 110:4. And the reasoning used by the author of Hebrews is not exactly a style of argument we're used to. Nevertheless, he uses Scripture to explain Scripture and reads the Old Testament verses in a way that points ahead to Jesus, establishing him as a better high priest than ever previously known. Rather than critique his style, we'll put our energy into understanding his argument as best we can. Here's a summary of the context in Genesis:

**GOING DEEPER**

Melchizedek was a priest-king of the city Salem, who met Abraham as he returned from routing certain invading kings. In the Old Testament narrative four kings from the east ... marched on a confederation of five kings from Sodom, Gomorrah, Admah, Zeboiim, and Bela. The armies of the latter were defeated in a valley called Siddim and their cities plundered. Lot, Abraham's nephew, was among the captives taken from Sodom, a fact brought to the attention of the patriarch by a servant who had escaped the battle. Abraham pursued the invaders to Dan, where he staged a night-time attack, putting the enemies to flight and recovering their booty. After his return home both the king of Sodom and Melchizedek, priest of God Most High, met Abraham. The author of Hebrews focuses on Abraham's encounter with the latter, in which Abraham gave a tithe and received a blessing.[4]

*"You are a priest forever, in the order of Melchizedek" (Ps. 110:4).*

4. What can we glean about the genealogy of Melchizedek from Genesis 14:17–20 and Psalm 110:4? How does the author of Hebrews use this scanty information to classify Jesus as the same kind of priest (7:3)?

① He blessed Abram
God called Melchizedek 'Most High'
② He was without mother, father, or descent

5. The author of Hebrews credits Melchizedek with greatness because Abraham gave him a portion (a tithe, or tenth) of the plunder from his battle. Can you follow his argument in 7:4–10? What reasons does he give for considering Melchizedek greater than the Levitical priests?

## JESUS, THE GREATEST HIGH PRIEST[5]

*Read Hebrews 7:11–28.*

6. We are reminded in 7:19 that the goal of having a priesthood was for people to draw near to God. There was certainly an elaborate system established by God and carried out by the Levitical priests to accomplish that. Why was there a need for a priest who was not of the Levites (7:11, 18–19)?

for a better hope

Gal 2:25

7. According to each of the following verses, how specifically is Jesus qualified for a better priesthood than the Levites?

7:16 *He is the power of an endless life*

7:19 *He is a better hope*

7:21 *He had an oath — Thou art a priest for ever after the order of Melchisedec*

7:24 *He continueth for ever, hath an unchangeable Priesthood*

7:25 *He is able to save us & to make intercession for man*

7:27 *He offered himself up for our sins*

Jesus is able to "save completely those who come to God through him." That is, since Christ's priesthood lasts forever, there are no limitations on the mediation he offers between us and God. His priestly ministry brings a complete salvation in that it not only offers temporary deliverance from sin, but perfects those who come to God through him for all time (10:1–3).... [W]e could not hope to draw near eternally to the eternal God through a dead priest. In Jesus we have a priest who provides salvation for us perpetually and completely.[6]

**GOING DEEPER**

8. Let's take a moment to reflect here. The reason for having a priest is to allow us to draw near to God. Jesus is the best priest there could possibly be. Does it make a difference in your daily life? How might you be able to take better advantage of the fact that you have the Great High Priest available to you on a continual basis?

*He makes a difference in my daily life & I take advantage that I have the Great High Priest threw prayer*

# LET US DRAW NEAR[7]

*Read Hebrews 4:14 – 16 and 8:1 – 2.*

Think of these verses as bookends around our discussion on the priesthood. The author of Hebrews takes great care to explain the theological understanding of the priesthood, supporting it with concepts from the Old Testament. It's important to build our faith on a foundation of understanding and not just rely on emotions or feelings, which don't provide anchors during storms. What's more, the author wants our understanding to be put into faith and action, so he continues to intertwine exhortations with explanations. These verses should give legs to our thoughts on the priesthood.

9. Both 4:14 – 16 and 8:1 – 2 make reference to the fact that our High Priest is now in heaven, serving at the right hand of God in the true, heavenly tabernacle. What difference does it make that he is intimately familiar with both realms — the world in which we live and the realm of heaven where God dwells?

    *because we are living in the world so He understand the problems of the world and now He lives in Heaven where we want to go*

10. Because we have a High Priest who has gone through the heavens, we're told that we should hold firmly to our faith (4:14). To paraphrase, Jesus successfully walked the path laid out for him. How does that make a difference for us when we're going through tough times?

    *He understands us & we can ask for help*

11. The second exhortation we're given is to "approach God's throne of grace with confidence, so that we may receive mercy and find grace to help us in our time of need" (4:16). Most of us don't live in a monarchy these days, but we could imagine an audience with Queen Elizabeth of Great Britain. When you think of approaching a king on his throne, what sort of benefits might a king bestow that you don't normally have? How does a "throne of grace" make it easier to imagine approaching such a king with confidence?

*① a pardon*

*② with faith*

12. The image of approaching the throne was understood in the ancient world as a symbol for prayer.[8] List what the Great High Priest, Jesus, is specifically doing as he serves "in the sanctuary, the true tabernacle set up by the Lord, not by a mere human being" (8:2).

*interceding on our behalf*
*he has given his life for our sins*
*makes it possible to draw near in worship*
*of god*
*actively involved in training us to become*
*more like himself*

What sort of prayers do you suppose are like a sweet aroma, or music to his ears?

*prayers that express worship, confession,*
*thankfulness, frustration, fears, need*
*for guidance + daily provision, +*
*desire for change*

# RESPONDING TO GOD'S WORD

## IN YOUR GROUP:

Take turns praying Ephesians 3:14–21 aloud, substituting the name of someone in your group where the blanks indicate, until each person in your group has been prayed for once by name:

*For this reason I kneel before the Father, from whom every family in heaven and on earth derives its name. I pray that out of his glorious riches he may strengthen _____ with power through his Spirit in their inner being, so that Christ may dwell in their heart through faith. And I pray that _____, being rooted and established in love, may have power, together with all the Lord's people, to grasp how wide and long and high and deep is the love of Christ, and to know this love that surpasses knowledge—that _____ may be filled to the measure of all the fullness of God.*

*Now to him who is able to do immeasurably more than all we ask or imagine, according to his power that is at work within us, to him be glory in the church and in Christ Jesus throughout all generations, for ever and ever! Amen.*

## ON YOUR OWN:

This week as you participate in corporate worship at church, consciously evaluate your attitude toward worship. Are you drawing near to God? Are you getting distracted? How much do you focus on yourself compared to God? Think about ways you could improve any weak spots for the next time.

## NOTES

1. This section is based on NIVAC: Hebrews, 185–199.
2. Guthrie, 194.
3. This section is based on *NIVAC: Hebrews*, 252–263.
4. Guthrie, 253.
5. This section is based on *NIVAC: Hebrews*, 264–276.
6. Guthrie citing P. E. Hughes, 268.
7. This section is based on *NIVAC: Hebrews*, 173–184.
8. Guthrie, 180.

# ENCOURAGE ONE ANOTHER, FOR GOD IS FAITHFUL

## Hebrews 8:3–10:25

We pulled out a dinosaur of a computer from storage a few months back. Curiously enough, when we plugged it in, it still actually worked, although we had to rack our brains to remember the commands to open and operate programs—it was from before the days of the mouse. It still had information on it that was interesting to access—old letters that were a link to the past and reminders of our early days of parenting adventures. It revealed patterns of our lives that are still there as well as some things that have changed. It's hard to imagine using that system anymore (or even wanting to), but at the time we upgraded it was a struggle to make the switch to a new system. When you're used to the old ways, it's always tempting to go back until you're completely convinced that the new way is better. In the last session, we saw how the author of Hebrews made the case for Jesus being a better high priest than the Levitical high priest, but the next few chapters take it even further. The whole system, not just the priesthood, gets upgraded when Jesus comes on the scene.

# THE OLD WAY — A SHADOWY REFLECTION[1]

*Read Hebrews 8:3 – 9:7.*

It's easy for us to dismiss the old covenant as obsolete from our vantage point today. But we don't appreciate what that old system meant for people at the time Hebrews was written. The original audience was inclined to go back to the old ways, whether because of pressure from the community or government, or from familiarity with and love for the Jewish tradition.

1.  The author of Hebrews summarizes the old system of worship in 9:1 – 7. Why was the old system good news for the Israelites (e.g., Lev. 9:23 – 10:3; 16:20 – 25; Deut. 8)?

    *It gave them a way to worship that they was accustomed to and a way of sacrifice for their sins that they understood*

    *A visual way of removing their sin*

**GOING DEEPER**

The old covenant system of worship may seem formal and rigid. It certainly would not be deemed a "cutting-edge" model of worship for contemporary culture! But look beyond the ritualistic orientation of that system to its significance. The path of the priests from the outer court to the inner sanctuary paints a picture of movement toward God. The regulations provided a means of drawing near. In the Old Testament language of holiness and punishments we can miss the main point—God was at work, working out means for his people to live in intimacy with him.[2]

2. Jeremiah was written just about the time the Jews were to be exiled for their disobedience—it was the end of the nation of Israel as they knew it. How would Jeremiah's message, quoted in Hebrews 8:8–12, have brought hope to the Israelites of Jeremiah's time?

*God was giving them a new + better way to restore the love + forgiveness of god*

What do you learn about God's character from the quote?

*He wants a lasting relationship*

3. How does the author of Hebrews view the old covenant? Consider his descriptions of the old versus the new in 8:5, 13; 9:11, 23–24; and 10:1. What would it mean for those who originally heard his words to return to these ways?

*The old covenant was inadequate and repetious.*
*The new covenant was a better way*

## A NEW AND BETTER WAY[3]

*Read Hebrews 9:8–10:18.*

4. The new system makes the most sense when we understand what the old system failed to accomplish. According to the following verses, what were the shortcomings of the old covenant system of worship?

9:9–10, 13 It was external. It did nothing for man's guilt or conscience

10:1–4 They had to be repeated over + over

10:11 The priest was doing the same thing over + over + it did not take away the sin

5. In contrast to question 4, how did the ministry of Jesus fulfill God's requirements, paving the way for a new kind of relationship with God?

9:11, 24 It was not man made. Jesus was the Son of God

9:12, 14 It was the sacrifice of the perfect life of Jesus + did not have to be repeated

9:25–28 Jesus was sacrificed only once + took away sins for all men

10:5–10 Jesus fulfilled the requirement of the Old Law

10:12–14 After fulfilling the requirements Jesus sat at the right hand of God

6. The author of Hebrews says that the Holy Spirit himself testifies to the superiority of the new covenant (10:15). Looking over your answers to questions 4 and 5, how would you summarize the difference between the two covenants?

*It is everlasting + given to us by the perfect one*

**GOING DEEPER**

[T]he author wishes to crystallize for his hearers the effectiveness and finality of Christ's sacrifice. The hearers are in danger of turning their backs on their Christian commitment; but the author reminds them, in no uncertain terms, that in so doing they walk away from God's provision by which people may have a cleansed conscience and a healthy, permanent relationship with him. In the new covenant alone can one find a means for decisive forgiveness from sin and, thus, right relationship with God. The Scripture bears witness specifically that the old covenant system is shown up as defunct by the ministry of Jesus.[4]

7. Because of Jesus' perfect sacrifice, we have a clean conscience (9:14), have been made perfect, and are being made holy (10:14). Does this describe your experience, or do you still fall short and feel guilty at times? How would you explain this reality?

# IMPLICATIONS OF THE NEW AND IMPROVED COVENANT[5]

*Read Hebrews 10:19–25.*

8. In the old covenant system, only the priests had access to God's presence. According to 10:19–22, how has your access to God changed as a believer in Christ under the new covenant? Compare the preparations of the high priest to enter God's presence on the Day of Atonement (Lev. 16:2–7, 14–16, 23–25, 34) with the preparations our High Priest Jesus has made for us (Heb. 10:19–22) to enter the Most Holy Place. How are they similar? How are they different or better?

*# Peter 1:3-4*

*The old covenant only the High Priest could enter the Most Holy Place. He had to dress in a certain way, wash a certain way, make a burnt offering, sprinkle blood, + this was done only at certain time. In the new covenant everyone can talk to God any time*

9. Because we have this "new and living way" to enter into God's presence, how might our worship be different now compared to before Jesus' coming? Does your worship reflect the privileged position that has been made available for you?

*Everyone can enter God's presence any where and at any time with out ritual or blood*

10. Perseverance is a big theme in Hebrews. The author encourages us to "hold unswervingly to the hope we profess, for he who promised is faithful" (10:23). Is this something that's hard for you to do? What can you do now to prepare for a time when you might be tempted to "let go of the rope"?

*study the word*
*Pray*

GOING DEEPER

It takes resolve to live a "long obedience" to the call of God. To "hold unswervingly to the hope we profess" demands a mature response to the obstacles and oppositions built into the warp and woof of a fallen world rebelling against God. To "hold unswervingly" demands a choice to be faithful, but our hope is well-grounded in the faithfulness of God.... Ultimately we do not have the resources within ourselves to stay with the goal God has set before us. We must choose. We must tighten down our resolve. We must hold. But at the end of the day, we must rest in the goodness, the resolve, and the faithfulness of God, who has promised an inheritance to his children. We hold on even as he holds us and takes us all the way to the end of the path.[6]

11. The community of faith is not optional, according to the author of Hebrews. How does the exhortation to "spur one another on toward love and good deeds" (10:24) reflect a "new and improved" covenant community?

12. Would you characterize yourself as an encourager? What would those who interact with you on a regular basis say? How does this exhortation flow out of drawing near to God?

## RESPONDING TO GOD'S WORD

The movie *Waking Ned Devine* includes a scene in which a man inadvertently attends a funeral service intended for him (though he's not dead). He remarks on how nice it is to hear all the encouraging things the people from his village had to say about him when they thought he was dead. Too often we wait for moments like that to encourage those around us — whether we like them or not!

### IN YOUR GROUP:

Take a few minutes to share things you appreciate about the people in your group. Be creative! Maybe this can become a new habit.

### ON YOUR OWN:

Think about someone who has had a positive impact on your life or church, particularly someone you haven't seen in a while. Give them a call or write them a letter to let them know how they've made a difference in God's kingdom.

### NOTES

1. This section is based on *NIVAC: Hebrews*, 277–307.
2. Guthrie, 302.
3. This section is based on *NIVAC: Hebrews*, 308–339.
4. Guthrie, 330–331.
5. This section is based on *NIVAC: Hebrews*, 340–353.
6. Guthrie, 351–352.

# KEEP GOING: IT REALLY MATTERS!¹

## Hebrews 5:11 – 6:20; 10:26 – 39

The thing I love about children's sermons is the great word pictures they use to make a point stick in your head. I guess God knows we are all children at heart, and we sometimes need simple lessons, since he uses a lot of word pictures in Scripture to get his point across! For example:

> *"Land that drinks in the rain often falling on it and that produces a crop useful to those for whom it is farmed receives the blessing of God. But land that produces thorns and thistles is worthless and is in danger of being cursed. In the end it will be burned" (Heb. 6:7 – 8).*

We can spend an entire session debating theology, finer points, and implications, but a word picture like this is worth a thousand words — you get the gist in a moment (whether you like the message or not).

## GROWING UP IN FAITH²

*Read Hebrews 5:11 – 6:3.*

Notice that we've gone back to a text that was sandwiched between the discussions of Jesus being a high priest in the order of Melchizedek. The author of Hebrews suddenly changed gears, which was likely to rivet the attention of his hearers.[3] He's determined to get their full attention because this is an important warning for them all to hear.

1. The author of Hebrews creates another vivid word picture—what a baby feeds on—to convey maturity (or lack of it). According to 5:13–14, how does training in righteousness come about? Who is the teacher?

   *God is the teacher of righteousness.*

*"We have much to say about this, but it is hard to explain because you are slow [nothros] to learn" (Heb. 5:11 NIV).*

**GOING DEEPER**

[In Hebrews 5:11] the author articulates the slowness of learning of his readers with the [Greek word *nothros*]. In the ancient world ... [*nothros*] could mean "sluggish, dull, dimwit, negligent, lazy." It was used in extrabiblical literature, for example, of a slave with ears "stopped up" by laziness, who was thus not obedient instantly to the call of his master. In the sphere of athletics, the word could designate a competitor who was out of shape, lazy, and sluggish.... In other words, *nothros* connotes culpable negligence or sluggishness in some aspect of life.[4]

2. When I look back at old family pictures, I am usually surprised at how much my family has grown and changed. If you apply this to spiritual growth, would you feel the same way, or are you "sluggish" when it comes to change? Can you look back at certain points in your life and recognize how you've grown?

Would you consider yourself to be feeding on milk or solid food now? How do you see yourself growing spiritually in the future?

## A SEVERE WARNING[5]

*Read Hebrews 6:4–6 and 10:26–31.*

This is one of the most controversial sections of Scripture,[6] and we dare not pass over it or dismiss it lightly. If we don't take the warning to heart because we think it applies to someone else, we miss out on valuable teaching that was meant for our good.

3. Describe the characteristics of those who are being warned (6:4–5). Whom does it sound like the author of Hebrews is addressing?

*those already enlightened by the Word those who have tasted God Word and know of the world to come*

4. In light of the previous section (5:11 – 6:3), why is it particularly important to address the church about people who might fall away?

*Because it is so easy to fall away and so many people have fallen We need to always be prepared*

Is this a warning for some portion of the church or all of it?

*for all of the church*

**GOING DEEPER**

[P]articipation in the Christian community does not necessarily equal salvation. Just because a person starts well in his or her association with the church, we cannot afford to assume that finishing well will follow automatically; this places a great deal of responsibility both on us as individual Christians and on us as church leaders. As individuals we must rest in the grace and justice of God (6:10) even while we "show diligence to the very end" (6:11). As church leaders we are called to care for those who come into the church for spiritual nourishment and protection.[7]

5. Is the warning in these verses consistent with other portions of Scripture or is the author of Hebrews introducing a controversial new concept (see Num. 14:20 – 24; 1 Sam. 15:24 – 26; Matt. 13:18 – 23; 1 Cor. 10:6 – 12; 2 Peter 2:20 – 22)? *Rom 8: 27-31*

6. How does the author of Hebrews characterize the type of behavior that prohibits some from repenting and returning to the family of God (6:6b; 10:26, 29)?

*They are in sin + their judgement is worse*

7. What are the consequences for such actions according to 6:4–6 and 10:26–31?

*To sin + know God, law we suffer in guilt + in his judgement*

## CONFIDENCE IN THOSE WHO BELIEVE[8]

*Read Hebrews 6:9–12 and 10:35–39.*

Speaking the truth in love is a skill requiring guidance from the Holy Spirit — too often we do one at the expense of the other, with the result of hurting relationships through one extreme or the other. The author of Hebrews did not skimp on the truth in the last set of verses, but he tempers it now with his confidence in his audience. He allows them to search their own hearts, rather than judge them himself.

8. What is the source of the author's confidence in his "dear friends" (6:9–11)?

*The blood of Jesus gave us a better way*

9. The author of Hebrews uses the same Greek word *nothros* in 6:12, "we do not want you to become *lazy*," as he did in 5:11, "you are *slow* to learn" (NIV, italics added). Is he talking to the same people? Has something changed?

*It is unknown if he is talking to the same people but his message & warning is the same for everyone*

What must they/we do in order to avoid this description? Can you relate to such a struggle?

*We must persevere & heed his warning*

"However busy we may be, however mature and efficient we may seem, that growth, if we are real Christians, must go on. Even the greatest spiritual teachers, such as St. Paul and St. Augustine, could never afford to relax the tension of their own spiritual lives; they never seem to stand still, are never afraid of conflict and change. Their souls too were growing entities, with a potential capacity for love, adoration and creative service: in other words, for holiness, the achievement of the stature of Christ."[9]

## REAL-LIFE EXAMPLES[10]

*Read Hebrews 6:13–20 and 10:32–34.*

10. Examples from the past help to bolster our faith and remind us of who God wants us to be. Abraham is a fitting example here for struggling Christians. We know he had periods in his life when he faltered, such as the time he tried to fulfill God's promise of an heir in his own way, when Ishmael was conceived (Gen. 16). But the author of Hebrews is referring to a time of faith, when, after waiting twenty-five years for Isaac, Abraham obediently brought him to the region of Moriah to sacrifice him according to God's instruction (Gen. 22). What was Abraham's responsibility in this incident (Heb. 6:15)?

*To believe + obey*

What was God's role in this incident (6:17)?

*He made an oath + fulfilled it*

What can we learn from this interaction (6:19)?

*God makes a promise + we can believe him*

11. The author of Hebrews makes the claim that God's unchanging nature, confirmed ultimately in his provision of Jesus as the High Priest who offers a perfect sacrifice, gives us hope to anchor our lives (6:17–20). If you've ever been on a boat anchored on the water overnight, think about how important the anchor was in keeping you safe and secure. How does the hope that God has given through Jesus Christ provide security for life?

We can put our faith in god because he never fails us

GOING DEEPER

God says that life is *more* than what can be seen immediately, and he offers us a wealth of spiritual resources to be found in relation to Jesus Christ. Those spiritual resources are accessed as we trust God's Word and build our lives on it. His "oaths" help us to see beyond our limitations to his limitless power and provisions. Encouragement comes from knowing we play a part in a life both full of meaning and lasting. Thus our current circumstances can never adequately define who we are or what we are about.[11]

12. You've made it through the harshest warning section in Hebrews. In the end, does it make you feel discouraged because of your lack of maturity (5:11), or does it spur you on toward love and good deeds (10:24)? Explain.

66 / HEBREWS

# RESPONDING TO GOD'S WORD

## IN YOUR GROUP:

"Come, Thou Fount of Every Blessing"[12] is a traditional hymn that expresses the joy of knowing the grace of God mixed with the recognition that our hearts are prone to wander. In fact the hymn writer, Robert Robinson, was known to have wandered later in life when he came across the words he himself wrote and was struck anew by them.[13] It is a reminder that we are all in need of the warning given in Hebrews.

Sing together or listen to the hymn, thinking carefully about the words. Are you prone to wander? Share with the group what is helpful to pull you back on track.

> *Come, thou fount of every blessing,*
> *Tune my heart to sing Thy grace;*
> *Streams of mercy, never ceasing,*
> *Call for songs of loudest praise.*
> *Teach me some melodious sonnet,*
> *Sung by flaming tongues above.*
> *Praise the mount! I'm fixed upon it,*
> *Mount of Thy redeeming love.*
>
> *Jesus sought me when a stranger,*
> *Wandering from the fold of God;*
> *He, to rescue me from danger,*
> *Interposed His precious blood;*
> *How His kindness yet pursues me*
> *Mortal tongue can never tell,*
> *Clothed in flesh, till death shall loose me*
> *I cannot proclaim it well.*
>
> *O to grace how great a debtor*
> *Daily I'm constrained to be!*
> *Let Thy goodness, like a fetter,*
> *Bind my wandering heart to Thee.*
> *Prone to wander, Lord, I feel it,*
> *Prone to leave the God I love;*

*Here's my heart, O take and seal it,*
*Seal it for Thy courts above.*

## ON YOUR OWN:

Are there particular times in your life that you regret or feel bad about? Write them down on a piece of wood, then make a fire with them and watch them burn away. Prayerfully think about how they can be put behind you, as you enjoy the warmth of the flames. (If you don't have access to a fireplace, consider doing this with a piece of paper instead.)

## NOTES

1. My thanks to Thomas Keene for his timely lectures on Hebrews at Westminster Theological Seminary, giving me an overall understanding of the book at just the right time, and especially insight in regard to this session.
2. This section is based on *NIVAC: Hebrews*, 200–215.
3. Guthrie, 200.
4. Guthrie, 201–202.
5. This section is based on *NIVAC: Hebrews*, 216–223, 354–370.
6. See Guthrie, 216.
7. Guthrie, 232.
8. This section is based on *NIVAC: Hebrews*, 222–239, 360–370.
9. Guthrie quoting Evelyn Underhill, 364.
10. This section is based on *NIVAC: Hebrews*, 240–251, 358–359.
11. Guthrie, 248.
12. *http://www.cyberhymnal.org/htm/c/o/comethou.htm* (March 14, 2008).
13. *http://www.cyberhymnal.org/bio/r/o/b/robinson_r.htm* (March 14, 2008).

# RUN THE RACE: THE TORCH IS NOW YOURS!

## Hebrews 11:1 – 12:3

One of the experiences I cherish in my church is when there is a baptism. All eyes are focused on the pastor and the person being baptized. After questions have been answered and vows have been made, the pastor turns to the rest of the congregation and asks all who will assist in nurturing this new member of the family of faith to stand up. For me, it's an emotional moment to watch everyone get up. This is not some passive cheering section, but people of faith who will surround this individual to encourage, teach, admonish, and model what faith is all about. Hebrews reminds us that the "cloud of witnesses" aren't just people in our own times, but people who began carrying the torch in the race of faith many generations before us, pointing us to a faith we will begin to carry for ourselves as we grow.

## DEFINING FAITH[1]

*Read Hebrews 11:1 – 16.*

1. How does the author of Hebrews define faith (11:1)? How is "hope" used differently than in current common usage? Would you agree with his definition, or change or expand it somehow? Why or why not?

2. The author of Hebrews draws on numerous examples of biblical characters that his original audience would have been familiar with to make his point about faith. Rather than study each character extensively, let's look at what he says about faith through his examples. What do the following verses say to support or expand his definition of faith?

   11:3

   11:6

   11:7b

   11:10

   11:13

3. What themes, commonalities, or progressions do you see in the examples of faith in chapter 11 so far?

# FURTHER EXAMPLES OF FAITH[2]

*Read Hebrews 11:17–40.*

4. The author of Hebrews gives fewer explanations, but more examples of faith over the course of biblical history in the second half of the chapter. What is the overall impact of the chapter?

GOING DEEPER

For all its length, the chapter really presents us with a simple message that must not be missed: *The life of faith is the only life that pleases God.* The author uses the phrase "by faith" repeatedly throughout the chapter, calling the hearers to the manner by which one must live for God. The whole point of his example list is to provide voluminous evidence that faith is the posture by which people live lives of purposeful impact by and for God. We are convinced, as the original hearers certainly must have been, that these great heroes of faith are merely representatives of a much larger host to whom God has offered commendation.[3]

5. How might this chapter be a source of encouragement for the original audience, keeping in mind the persecution and difficult circumstances they could have been facing?

6. Although we think of the people listed in this chapter as heroes of the faith, there are certainly aspects of their lives that are not commendable. Noah was caught in a drunken stupor, Abraham put Sarah at risk when he lied saying she was his sister, Jephthah sacrificed his own daughter, David committed adultery and murder, to name a few. As human beings, they were all far from perfect, yet they are commended for their faith. What can we learn from this?

7. Are there other examples from the Bible or your own life that you would like to see included in this list? Explain why.

8. In 11:40, the author of Hebrews actually links the current audience together with the faithful of the past. What was the "something better" that God had planned? What characteristics do we have in common with the initial audience of the letter and the "hall of faith" examples?

## FIXING OUR EYES ON JESUS[4]

*Read Hebrews 12:1–3.*

Rather than thinking of the "hall of faith" examples like portraits on a wall that we can look at from time to time, the author of Hebrews wants them to be a constant, living reminder that influences how we think and go about our current lives.

9. How should chapter 11 motivate our race? What are the requirements for the race marked out for us (12:1)?

**GOING DEEPER**

This image of "running" emphasizes that Christ-followers have a course to complete or a goal to reach, and must exert effort if the Christian life is to be lived faithfully. The author has in view, however, a marathon rather than a sprint, as seen in the phrase "with endurance." The effort called for, consequently, is a sustained effort that goes the distance, following through on one's commitment with dogged determination. This is how we must run "the race marked out for us."[5]

10. In other sections of Hebrews, we've seen how the author uses comparisons of lesser and greater to make his point. Jesus is so much greater than the angels or Moses. His role as High Priest is so much more complete than that of the Old Testament high priests. Now we've been given clouds-worth of examples of faithful people, but once again, Jesus wins out, hands down. How is he a better example of faith than all the people mentioned in chapter 11?

11. Many times when I look at "heroes" of faith, I desire the character and maturity I see in them, but I don't relish the suffering they went through to become who they are. Jesus himself tells us there's a high cost to following him (for instance see Luke 14:25 – 35). How can fixing our eyes on Jesus help us to not grow weary or lose heart (Heb. 12:3)?

12. Consider your own race, marked out for you by your heavenly Father. What are the distractions along the way that prevent your eyes from being fixed on Jesus? What things hinder or easily entangle you, that you need to consider throwing off?

## RESPONDING TO GOD'S WORD

*IN YOUR GROUP:*

Set up "accountability partners" for a week, or even a month. Are there others in your group who had similar struggles as you in question 12 regarding distractions in your walk of faith? Pair up and pray for your partner, checking in periodically to encourage each other in your struggles. As a reminder, exchange coffee mugs with that person for the time that you are partners so that you can remember to pray for them whenever you are having a hot drink.

*ON YOUR OWN:*

Interview a retired person whom you know to be a Christian. Ask him or her about lessons of faith they have learned during their lives.

## NOTES

1. This section is based on *NIVAC: Hebrews*, 371–379.
2. This section is based on *NIVAC: Hebrews*, 379–394.
3. Guthrie, 386.
4. This section is based on *NIVAC: Hebrews*, 395–400, 405–406, 410–411.
5. Guthrie, 398.

# BE HOLY: GOD WILL BE PLEASED

## Hebrews 12:4–17; 13:1–25

Discipline is one of those words we tend to have a love-hate relationship with. We love to see the results of it—think of what it means for diet, exercise, study habits, behavior, our speech, and other aspects of relationships. There's little in life that it doesn't affect. But few of us really relish the process—whether we're on the giving or receiving end of things. Though we think of discipline most often connected with raising children, it's really a lifelong process that we never completely get away from. How natural, then, for the author of Hebrews to conclude his letter with practical guidelines for putting our faith into action with a discussion of discipline and respect for those who encourage it.

## GOD DISCIPLINES HIS CHILDREN[1]

*Read Hebrews 12:4–13.*

1. This is not the first time the author of Hebrews has referred to the immaturity of his audience. In 5:11 – 14 he compared them to infants still feeding on milk, not solid food. His comment in 12:4 reminds me of the maxim I heard repeatedly when growing up, in response to my various hurts and struggles: "You'll live to be a grandma!" How does the author put the hardships of his readers in perspective in 12:4 – 13?

*"God whispers to us in our pleasure, speaks in our conscience, but shouts in our pains: it is His megaphone to rouse a deaf world."*

C. S. Lewis

2. The picture conjured by the author in 12:12 – 13 goes back to the idea of running a race (12:1). You might not like being described as having feeble arms and weak knees, but the author could be referring to Isaiah 35:3 – 8. Who, according to Isaiah 35:8, is qualified to run their race on the Way of Holiness? Who performs most of the action in Isaiah 35:3 – 8?

3. What are the benefits of discipline according to Hebrews 12:5 – 11?

GOING DEEPER
In the cultural context behind Hebrews (both in Judaism and the broader Greco-Roman culture) the father was seen as having the ultimate responsibility for the training of a son.... Although a tutor might be responsible for the care and training of a boy after age six or seven, the ongoing role of the father was much more significant (cf. 1 Cor. 4:15). In a positive sense, the father's responsibility was to train his son in such a way that he was well prepared for adulthood. This training often involved correction and punishment, but the goal was to help the child develop character and wisdom.[2]

4. By now we should be familiar with the argument of from lesser to greater. Regardless of your experience with your own father, God's role as disciplinarian should be viewed as essential for our development into legitimate children of his. Think of some of the experiences in your life that have developed your character. How have these lessons exceeded things your parents taught you?

## LIVING HOLY LIVES[3]

*Read Hebrews 12:14–17 and 13:1–6.*

When the author of Hebrews talked about maturity in 5:14, he said that people trained themselves to distinguish good from evil. The verses in this section allow us to "practice" the skills of the faith we've been learning about throughout the book of Hebrews so we can grow in maturity.

5. Part of running the race marked out for us involves "throwing off everything that hinders and the sin that so easily entangles" (12:1). What things described in 12:14–17 and 13:1–6 fall into the category of hindrances or sin? How would they hamper your maturity as a Christian? How might you "throw them off"?

6. Looking at the same verses (12:14–17 and 13:1–6), which things describe actions or attitudes that we can "practice" as we keep our eyes fixed on Jesus? Are these things you actually integrate into your daily life, or just things you think about in theory? What would it take for you to improve in some of the areas?

**GOING DEEPER**

In areas such as marriage and money the worlds of the spirit and the street meet. Such meeting places either become dance floors on which we move to the music of his will or a stage of games on which we play at Christianity with dichotomized, hypocritical hearts. Everyday. Everyday. God wants us and wants us to want him in the nitty-gritty wonder, the plain and exalted dance of everyday.[4]

7. Fortunately, we're not left on our own for self-improvement. The true power behind Christianity lies in the fact that God has broken into our world of "self" to help us when we are incapable of helping ourselves. What reassurance does the author of Hebrews give of this (13:5–6)? Do you see any evidence of this making a difference in the lives of Christians compared to non-Christians? Why or why not?

8. Attempting to live a holy life pleasing to God assumes that we *want* to "grow up" in his family and inherit his blessings. As we've seen in other sessions, the consequences are severe for rejecting such an inheritance. How does the example of Esau bring this lesson home (12:16–17)?

## RESPECTING LEADERS[5]

*Read Hebrews 13:7–25.*

9. One further aspect of respecting God's discipline in our lives is submitting to the authorities he has put over us. According to 13:7–8, 17–18, what benefits do we potentially receive from church leaders? How can we assist them in doing their jobs well?

Church life is difficult. Relationships get strained because the church is full of real people. But when church leaders lead well, living lives worthy of imitation, and when church members follow their lead, the kingdom is built. God is pleased. This helps and benefits all.[6]

10. Hebrews 13:9 – 16 hints at inappropriate teachings or practices that may have involved some of the original readers. Perhaps some were being drawn back to traditional Jewish ceremonies. How might some well-intended ceremonial practices have been a hindrance to the race of faith for those early Christians?

What is the author's antidote for such practices?

11. Are there aspects of your worship that are done purely for tradition or conformity with others — things that might actually sidetrack you from focusing on Jesus?

What does it look like for you to continually offer to God a sacrifice of praise — the fruit of lips that confess his name, and activities that do good for others?

12. How does the author's benediction (13:20 – 21) summarize the "short" letter he has written (v. 22)?

Is there one particular aspect of this benediction that speaks most loudly to you?

*"Now may the God of peace, who through the blood of the eternal covenant brought back from the dead our Lord Jesus, that great Shepherd of the sheep, equip you with everything good for doing his will, and may he work in us what is pleasing to him, through Jesus Christ, to whom be glory for ever and ever. Amen" (Heb. 13:20 – 21).*

# RESPONDING TO GOD'S WORD

## IN YOUR GROUP:

Decide on a group project you can do together that would encourage and bless your church leadership, such as a night out for the pastor (including babysitting if necessary), a week of meals, notes of encouragement, etc.

## ON YOUR OWN:

Read Isaiah 35:3 – 10. Take some time to pray:

- Confess ways you need to strengthen your feeble hands and knees that give way.
- Give thanks for the way God has cleansed you and equipped you to walk in his Way.
- Praise God, who will transform our broken world and circumstances to great joy and blessing.

## NOTES

1. This section is based on *NIVAC: Hebrews*, 395 – 415.
2. Guthrie, 407.
3. This section is based on *NIVAC: Hebrews*, 433 – 438, 447 – 450.
4. Guthrie, 450.
5. This section is based on *NIVAC: Hebrews*, 438 – 447, 450 – 452.
6. Guthrie, 452.

# LEADER'S NOTES

## SESSION 1 LEADER'S NOTES

1. This sampling shows the great variety of ways God spoke through his prophets—direct revelation, visions, dreams, fire and smoke, use of common elements, nature, life experiences, and miracles, to name a few. Although these events might seem rather dramatic, they were mysterious and partial. God's story and purposes were gradually revealed throughout Old Testament times, but became much clearer when he spoke directly through his Son. His message consistently offered both blessings for obedience and curses for disobedience, but the character and scope of his kingdom were revealed more clearly through Jesus, and ultimately when Jesus fulfilled the Father's plans through his death and resurrection.

2. • Jesus is God's Son, and as such, is the heir of all things.
   • The universe was created through Jesus and is sustained by him.
   • Jesus exactly represents God to us, the "radiance of God's glory."
   • He came to earth in order to cleanse us from sin.
   • He is seated at the right hand of God and is superior to angels.
   • These things give us a clearer understanding of God than all the "various ways" before, since Jesus was God himself in the flesh.

3. The superiority and importance of Jesus has to be a main focus, based on this introduction. The comparison between Old Testament and New Testament times is key as well, especially comparing Jesus' role, which is more glorious and complete than the old system could offer. Perseverance in faith over the long haul is another important theme, though more subtle in the introduction.

4. The more specific you are here, the more helpful this will be to you. For example, someone who has trouble relating to God might focus on the fact that Jesus is the exact representation of his being, and look at more passages about Jesus to understand what God is like. Someone who struggles with anxiety might want to remind herself of how Jesus sustains all things — there are no circumstances out of his control. Purification for sins is another way of looking at the grace of forgiveness — a free gift that covers all sin, whether arguments with someone we love or work with, failure to live up to expectations, ways we have hurt others, etc.

5. The author assumes that Scripture is the very Word of God and that it is true. He also assumes that the message of the Old Testament is consistent with the message of Christ and that the Scripture of the Old Testament is pointing ahead, witnessing to the coming of Christ. Furthermore, there is an expectation that these Scriptures would be familiar to the readers. Quoting a couple of lines would likely make them think of the whole context or psalm. These are very different assumptions from most of the world today, where human thought is usually valued higher than God's thoughts, and truth is thought of as relative. Most people today are not familiar with the Scriptures quoted, and have to work harder to understand them in context. That said, the assumptions being made are sound theologically and give Christians today a strong foundation and example in how to study and understand the Scriptures.

6. There's clearly a close relationship — an intimacy — between Father and Son that cannot be broken (Ps. 2:7). The Lord and his Anointed One (Ps. 2:2) are on the same side against the kings and rulers of the earth. When threatened by the nations, God just laughs. Nothing can change the fact that he has installed his Son as King — God can do whatever he wants to accomplish.

7. God's plan was in place before the beginning of time. God tells David of this plan (although Solomon was the immediate fulfillment) a thousand years before Christ came to earth. A thousand years might be a moment to God, but it's incredible to think about him talking about his plans for Jesus so long before it happens—and then bringing them to pass! God's plans for Jesus are clearly much more central to his kingdom than angels, though the angels certainly have their place.

8. Angels are servants of God: worshiping him and his Son, acting as messengers on behalf of God, and protecting God's people. These are important roles, but nothing in comparison to the role of the King who rules the universe.

9. The king described is majestic, splendid, and the most excellent of men. He is a powerful and victorious king, yet he stands for truth, humility, and righteousness. There seems to be no doubt that his reign will never end—good news that couldn't be said about earthly kingdoms! The kingdom is characterized by righteousness and justice, and has therefore gotten the wholehearted approval of God himself. Who wouldn't want to live in a kingdom like this?

10. Unlike people, whose days vanish like smoke (Ps. 102:3), Jesus will remain forever, never changing. He took part in creating the heavens and earth, and will be there when they end. Humanity on the earth, as part of creation, will change like clothing that wears out and is discarded, but Jesus is of a different nature that will never end or change.

11. The warning here and throughout Hebrews is unmistakable: drifting away from an understanding of God and his purposes for your life has severe consequences. At the same time, knowing that we have a King who is victorious, whose enemies will become a footstool for Jesus' feet, should give great hope. The struggle we face is temporary and the outcome has already been determined. That doesn't give us any guarantees about our individual lives and immediate difficulties, but puts things into perspective—which should provide comfort as well as the challenge to persevere.

12. The authority of Jesus is unmistakable. If we believe Scripture to be true, there should be no doubt in our minds that worship and obedience to our King are not only required and appropriate, but a privilege in light of the kind of King we serve.

# SESSION 2 LEADER'S NOTES

1. Hebrews 2:5 summarizes what the author was talking about in 1:5 – 14, namely that the world is subject to Jesus, not to the angels. Angels are just servants of God, whereas Jesus is the Son and inheritor of all things.

2. Jesus is described as being made a little lower than the angels, or as Guthrie's quote following this question points out, was made lower than the angels for a little while. This is quite a switch from the emphasis in the previous chapter about how much more exalted Jesus is compared to the angels. It does not refer to the "essence" or character of Jesus changing, but that he willingly subjected himself to being human for this time period, as described also in Philippians 2:6 – 11. Jesus willingly suffered in this manner so that by the grace of God he might taste death for everyone (Heb. 2:9).

3. This is not a contradiction, but an introduction of the concept of the "already-not-yet." We, like the original audience of Hebrews, live in a time period where Jesus' work has *already* been accomplished, but at the same time the full realization of his kingdom has *not yet* happened. Jesus is King of the universe, and everything is subject to him, but at present we are engaged in skirmishes with the sin that remains — which will be true until he returns. We still suffer, but knowing it is expected and temporary should be comforting. It explains why bad things still happen, but it does not negate the work that Jesus has already accomplished; in fact we will see shortly how suffering is actually purposeful in our lives — and how it points ahead to a future hope.

4. • God was bringing many sons and daughters to glory (2:10).
   • Jesus' brothers and sisters are being made holy (2:11).
   • Jesus' death frees those who all their lives were held in slavery by their fear of death (2:15).
   • It is Abraham's descendants who are helped (2:16). (Abraham is the father of those people who believe God and are declared righteous on the basis of faith in him.)
   • Jesus made atonement for the sins of the people (2:17).
   • Jesus is able to help those who are being tempted (2:18).

   It's rather humbling to consider all the help we need, but honoring as well that God would raise us to such a level of glory and holiness! As we consider what Jesus went through, it should also give us a sense of awe that Jesus was willing to suffer and even die a horrible death in order to do all of these things for us.

5. Hebrews 2:10 says that it was fitting for God to make Jesus, the one who wrote the book on salvation, to be made perfect through suffering. He was not ashamed to call us brothers and sisters since he is of the same family (2:11). Jesus had to learn what it means to trust God (2:13). Hebrews 2:14, 17, and 18 emphasize that Jesus was made human like us in every way. He shared in the experience of being human and in all the difficulties that go with it—especially facing temptation, suffering, and death.

6. In Hebrews 2:12, quoting Psalm 22:22, Jesus calls us his brothers and sisters, and places himself in our midst "in the presence of the congregation" (NIV). Likewise, in Hebrews 2:13, quoting Isaiah 8:18, as the children God has given him, we are part of the same family. The fact that we all must trust God (2:13) also puts us and Jesus in the same position of dependence on God. This sense of brotherhood creates a sense of intimacy between God and humanity that makes Christianity unique among the world's religions.

7. Think specifically about situations in which these types of scenarios may have been true for you. Although Jesus' life cannot parallel every single experience a given individual has had, his human experience equips him to understand the same longings, temptations, joy, and suffering in everything you go through. Consider the fact that he grew up in a family that may have been marginalized, that he knew hunger and betrayal, that he was abandoned by friends, tempted, abused, beaten, that he suffered injustice, and experienced the loss of loved ones. If you've never thought of relating to him in this manner, consider what it means to turn to him in prayer—in addition to others around you—for comfort.

8. Most belief systems are impersonal and, in essence, require us to try harder, to find it in ourselves to improve and lift up ourselves to the level that God or religion requires. In contrast, the God of Christianity, in his great mercy and love, stoops down to our level and gets intimately involved with us, bringing a power we ourselves do not have, to destroy even the things that seem to have power over us—namely, sin and death.

9. We are called "holy brothers and sisters." That means that "the one who makes people holy" (2:11) accomplished his goal. Just as he "who was made

lower than the angels for a little while [is] now crowned with glory and honor" (2:9), so we follow after and share in the heavenly calling. What a great deal for us!

10. There are two aspects that come to mind regarding "fixing our thoughts on Jesus." One is the aspect of gratitude for what he has done for us. We who were anything but holy now have a heavenly calling and are intimately connected with our holy God. We need to remind ourselves continually about what that means in our lives. Secondly, as we follow after Jesus, we are called to live holy lives, striving to act according to the holy family we are a part of, following in the steps of our "big brother."

11. As the Creator, rather than the created, Jesus is in a superior position. Jesus is privy to all knowledge, whereas Moses only knew in a limited way what God had revealed to him. Jesus is also the essence of what humanity should be like, whereas Moses, though a faithful servant, was still sinful and bound to death. Ultimately, Jesus has the privileges of a son, whereas Moses is considered a mere servant to the son.

12. Answers will vary, but we certainly know family members more intimately. That can be a detriment if it isn't Jesus we're talking about! But knowing a person intimately gives us a better chance of being able to follow in his or her footsteps. In fact, we're more likely to imitate that person without realizing it when they are part of our lives day in and day out. We might also get support or encouragement from that person along the way. This has interesting parallels for thinking about following Jesus. For the original audience of Hebrews, following Jesus also gets Gentile Christians out of the dilemma of not knowing as much about Moses as Jewish Christians, or not feeling connected to him through Jewish family lines.

# SESSION 3 LEADER'S NOTES

1. In Psalm 95:8, the incident referred to as "rebellion" in Hebrews 3:8 and 15 is the grumbling of the desert wanderers for water. The place where Moses struck the rock was called Meribah ("quarreling") and Massah ("testing") to commemorate the quarreling of the people as they tested God. In the books of Exodus and Numbers, the Israelites were continually grumbling against God about food, water, other general hardships, having to wait too long for Moses at Mount Sinai (the golden calf incident), and discovering that God's Promised Land for them was full of people they were too scared to fight. They continually reasoned from a state of distrusting God and his promises, despite the many miracles he demonstrated on their behalf, and they either tried to take things into their own hands, or grumbled about what they could not change, wishing for the "comforts" they had in their former slavery. Given these examples, rebellion seems to be a fair description of their overall attitude.

2. Living in the desert for forty years was no piece of cake, but the Israelites asked for it. Their deliverance from Egypt should have been proof enough of God's miraculous powers, but they immediately called that into question after they got across the Red Sea. If they had trusted in God's promises from the beginning, as Caleb and Joshua did, they never would have had to experience the forty years in the desert. But even there, God provided for them miraculously on a daily basis. Nevertheless, they hardened their hearts, just as Pharaoh did in Egypt, and were judged for it. None of the original generation made it out of the desert to the promised rest because of their disobedience.

3. The author of Hebrews is warning his readers against having "a sinful, unbelieving heart that turns away from the living God" (3:12). In any congregation, there is a mix of heart attitudes, and there is always a risk of people drifting or falling away. Keep in mind that this is addressed corporately to the church, and God alone truly knows the hearts of those around us. He is warning believers to examine their own hearts and to persevere to the end. Encouraging one another to stay focused on Christ's work is necessary to keep from falling away.

4. The dangers of drifting are just as high today as they were when Hebrews was written. In fact, in today's fast-paced culture, perseverance and commitment over the long haul are not really "in style," which makes the message particularly relevant, even if unpopular. The message we sometimes get of "once saved, always saved" does not actually reflect the tension throughout Scripture between the assurance of salvation and the need to persevere to the end. As Guthrie says, "the drifter in a state of drifting has no assurance of his or her right standing before God."[1] Sin has been and always will be deceitful, so we have to be wary of hardening our hearts, grumbling against God's will, or taking things into our own hands, just like the desert wanderers did.

5. Responses will vary since this is a very personal question, and some people might be hesitant to answer (be sensitive to this in a group setting). However, a little familiarity with Scripture should put everyone on the same page for "There is no one righteous, not even one; there is no one who understands, there is no one who seeks God. All have turned away, they have together become worthless; there is no one who does good, not even one" (Rom. 3:10–12). Honest reflection should reveal hearts that are not right, except through the righteousness of Christ.

6. In Leviticus, the Sabbath rest is linked to the Day of Atonement, when the sacrifice made once a year for sin cleansed the people and no one was allowed to work. This points ahead to the sacrifice of Jesus which we cannot work for, and which cleanses from sin for all time all who put their faith in him. This is the heart of the gospel preached to us since Jesus came to earth. The weekly practice of Sabbath on Sunday, the day Jesus rose from the dead, commemorates his sacrifice that saves us.

7. "[R]esting from one's own work . . . does not mean a cessation of effort but rather an obedient, active dependence on God."[2] We experience this rest now when we rest from our efforts to earn salvation — it is a gift we receive in faith. To enjoy the freedom that God's forgiveness provides gives us a peace and joy that would be out of reach for us otherwise. But we can also look forward to a future rest, where we will be fully in communion with God and will no longer need to make the effort to fight sin and its effects in this world.

8. Entering God's rest does not mean taking a break from work or from our usual activities one day a week, although that is important. To enter God's rest does not mean to do our best to keep his commandments or to do good deeds. To enter God's rest means to live out of a place of faith in Christ. We must know him and his Word well enough that we can see ourselves through his eyes and respond by living accordingly. Our busy lives often make it difficult to rest in the way God wants us to. We must humble ourselves and trust in his forgiveness instead of our own means for justifying our actions—and then act in obedience. These things should be done individually, but also in the context of a church community where we can "encourage one another daily" (3:13).

9. The warnings in Hebrews 3–4 were serious enough—death in the desert, and no rest in the Promised Land; how could it be any worse? But the judgment described in 12:25–27 encompasses a shake-up of all of creation—there's no escape for anyone! Better to heed the warning and act "Today," before it's too late. None of us knows when that final shake-up will be.

10. The contrast between the two mountains is dramatic. Worship at Mount Sinai, as described in 12:18–21, was impersonal, filled with terror, and threatened condemnation. Even Moses, the servant of God, was terrified. Approaching God meant death. Worship at Mount Zion, or the heavenly Jerusalem, according to 12:22–24, is full of joy and excitement. Believers along with angels can approach God's throne in joyful worship, thanks to the grace shown us through the sacrifice of Jesus' blood.

11. From the very beginning, God has been clear about both the blessings of obedience and the curses for disobedience. Because he is both just and loving, we must keep both holiness and mercy together. Knowing and trusting in the God who watches over us cannot help but lead to worship. But going our own way cannot help but end in destruction. We were made as creatures dependent on the living God.

12. Remember that worship begins as an attitude in your own heart. Sometimes the way you regard what's going on around you simply reflects your own attitude, not what's actually happening. This is not a question about the style of worship, but the attitude of worship.

# NOTES

1. Guthrie, 142–143.
2. Guthrie, 157.

# SESSION 4 LEADER'S NOTES

1. A priest is an intermediary appointed to represent the people to God and God to his people. A priest offers gifts and sacrifices on behalf of the people to deal with their sins so they can approach God, and he gently deals with people who are ignorant or going astray — in other words, he teaches them what God expects of them if they wish to be people of God.

2. Because of the sin that originated in the garden of Eden, the relationship between God and people was critically damaged. Instead of walking with God, as was originally established, Adam and Eve hid from God. Moses' response was similar — the holiness of God created a fear that humankind could no longer bridge because of their sin. Nevertheless, God continued to watch over and hear the cries of his people. His desire was to care for them and restore a relationship with them. Eventually he established a priesthood through which the people were invited to know and worship the God who loved them.

3. The description in Hebrews is pretty basic: the high priest had to be a man, but he had to be called by God. Other descriptions in the Old Testament point out that it was a position unique to the tribe of Levi, descendants of Aaron, and that the eldest son became high priest when his father, the previous high priest, died. We learned in Hebrews 2 that Jesus became like us in every way possible, so that he could sympathize with our weaknesses. Without suffering as a human, Jesus would not have qualified for the job. The author of Hebrews emphasizes this again in 5:7–9. But Jesus' calling to the priesthood is different from that of ancient Israel's high priest. Hebrews 5:5 says he was declared to be God's Son (quoting Ps. 2:7) and Hebrews 5:6 declares him a priest (quoting Ps. 110:4), but a priest in the order of Melchizedek, not of Aaron, so he was uniquely qualified (more on that in the next section).

4. The author of Hebrews is not saying that Melchizedek actually lived eternally, but that his priesthood was dissimilar to that of the Levitical priests of Israel in two important ways. There is no information about Melchizedek's birth or death presented in Scripture, which suggests that his priesthood was not based on father-to-son succession like the Levitical priests. Secondly, by this "argument of silence,"[1] Melchizedek's priesthood

was not constrained by the boundary of death like the Levitical priests. Jesus' priesthood is also not based on having been born into the priestly tribe (for he wasn't), and his priesthood is truly eternal by virtue of his resurrection. The priesthood of Jesus is therefore similar in these ways to the order of Melchizedek (Ps. 110:4).

5. Because the Levites were descended from Abraham, the fact that Abraham gave a tithe (tenth) to Melchizedek makes him greater. If we give an offering to a governor, but the governor in turn gives the offering to a president or king, we would consider the president or king the highest in the line of command. The argument is similar here. In addition, the Levitical priests die, whereas there is no mention of the death of Melchizedek, so his priesthood is considered timeless.

6. Hebrews 7:18 states that the former regulation is set aside because it was weak and useless. That's not to say that God tried "plan A" and it didn't work, so he went to his fallback "plan B." The original priesthood was never intended to perfectly restore the relationship between God and his people. In God's unfolding plan, he created a system that allowed his people to begin to know his ways and to worship him in a true bit limited way. That system pointed out their *inability* to know him fully and pointed toward the One who would make it possible to restore them fully as his children and heirs, enabling them to walk again in his presence with a deeper relationship than ever before.

7. 7:16 — Jesus is chosen as priest because of his eternal life, not because he was born into a certain tribe.

7:19 — Jesus introduces a greater hope of drawing near to God, perpetually.

7:21 — God made an oath that Jesus would be a priest forever, guaranteeing a better covenant since God does not change his mind.

7:24 — Because Jesus won't die, he offers permanent salvation for us.

7:25 — Because Jesus won't die, he completes our salvation for us — he can always intercede for us, so the process of changing us can be finished.

7:27 — Because Jesus was perfect and sinless, he only had to sacrifice once for all, not continually.

8. Take some time to reflect on this during the week. Answers will vary of course, but consider what it means to really get to know God better — that

can happen through reading about him, praying to him, and understanding the powerful spiritual resources he makes available when we step out beyond our own abilities and lean on him. Then of course there are the times that we fall short—are we turning to him for forgiveness, learning through our experiences, expressing thanks for his care over us? These should not be isolated "religious" experiences, but part of our day-to-day struggles as we learn to turn to our High Priest, Jesus, to continually teach us more about God and what he expects of us.

9. As Hebrews 4:16 suggests, Jesus' priesthood should give us greater confidence before God. We know we are being accurately represented because Jesus knows what it's like to be in our shoes. At the same time, we can trust what he says to be true since he represents the workings of the heavenly kingdom. Knowing the Son is like having an "in" with the most powerful authority there is, given his privilege and favor with God the Father. Just think how much easier it is to go into an unfamiliar situation if you know someone on the inside who is willing to speak up for you and can lead you through all the appropriate steps or places.

10. Jesus sets an example for us. He was faced with all kinds of difficulties and temptations, but persevered obediently to the end; he never threw in the towel or decided to do things his own way to avoid suffering. So we can't say he doesn't understand (4:15). It is possible to live through difficulties with a godly perspective, though it can certainly be a challenge. Because Jesus has gone through this earthly life successfully, it should also give us perspective on the temporary nature of our times. We can have stability in the midst of our chaotic world when we view life from the perspective of eternity.

11. A king is generally known for both resources and authority that common people wouldn't have. But a king's resources and authority might also cause fear. Therefore, approaching a "throne of grace" sounds pretty wonderful. Jesus has already saved us from any possible condemnation by sacrificing his own life (see Rom. 8:31–39). The worst that can happen when we approach the throne of grace is that we are given "no" as an answer, which is sometimes in our best interests anyway.

12. As Jesus performs his duties as our priest in heaven:

- he is constantly interceding on our behalf;
- he has given his life for our sins;

- he makes it possible for us to draw near in worship of God;
- he is actively involved in training us to become more like himself.

God is happy to hear all our prayers, big and small. But without careful consideration, our prayers sometimes turn into "laundry lists," or they become dry and rote. Studying prayers in the Bible is a great way to learn what kind of prayers please God but, no matter what language we use, our prayers should always be from the heart. And they should include a variety of interactions with God, similar to our conversations with other people. Expressing worship, confession, thankfulness, frustration, fears, the need for guidance or daily provision, and a desire for change (in ourselves and others) are among the many examples of prayers throughout the Bible.

## NOTE

1. See Guthrie, 254.

# SESSION 5 LEADER'S NOTES

1. The law was necessary to make clear what was acceptable to a holy God and what was not — it defined what obedience meant. The old covenant system for worship was very welcome to the Jews because it provided a means for them to remember the nature of their God and draw near to him (i.e., worship him) and deal with their sin (i.e., their failures to uphold the law). But a lot of fear surrounded this approach to a holy and active God. What a relief it must have been to have priests as intermediaries (and what a scary job for the Levites)!

2. Israel's disobedience should have incurred their total destruction by God. Instead, he's offering hope through a new covenant that promises restoration and forgiveness. God's justice is evident — he did get angry and turn away from his disobedient people — but his mercy and love come out even more strongly, offering them a new and better way in which they will know him better and he will forgive them.

3. The old covenant was a prototype for the new covenant. Like a poster of a real painting, it gave a good idea of what to expect, but it was a shadowy reflection of the real thing. To stick with the old would mean shortchanging oneself of all the benefits of the new — namely a relationship with God and forgiveness of sins. It would mean returning to a life characterized by a fear of God that would ultimately be futile, since Hebrews 8:13 points out that what is obsolete will disappear. (Besides, the old system of sacrifice would soon be impossible to perform — the temple in Jerusalem was destroyed by the Romans in AD 70.) Even what the old system offered in limited ways would be gone since it was replaced with the new covenant. To worship the old way would simply be an ineffective memory of the past.

4. 9:9 – 10, 13 — The sacrifices that were offered could only provide external cleansing; they could do nothing to clear a guilty conscience.

   10:1 – 4 — The sacrifices were inadequate — they had to be performed over and over again. They could remind people of their sins, but not take them away permanently.

   10:11 — Because of the inadequacy of the sacrifices and the need to perform them again and again, the priest's job was never done — he had to always remain standing, day after day. There was no rest for him or the people.

5. 9:11, 24 — Jesus' ministry was accomplished in the heavenly tabernacle, not the man-made version on earth, so he had direct access to God, and could represent us there.

9:12, 14 — He sacrificed his own blood, not that of animals, and because of the perfect life he led here, it bought us "eternal redemption," that is, it could actually cleanse our consciences of guilt for all time. It also enabled us to serve the living God instead of just ourselves.

9:25 – 28 — Jesus only had to suffer and offer his blood once, not repeatedly like the earthly priests' sacrifices. Because it was such a superior sacrifice, it did away with sin once and for all, and for all people.

10:5 – 10 — Although God established the Law, it was never intended to fully solve the problem of humanity's sin. It was God's plan from the beginning, and his will, to have Jesus fulfill his requirements on the cross (cf. Acts 4:27 – 28).

10:12 – 14 — Jesus was able to *sit* at the right hand of God and rest, having accomplished what he was intended to do, in contrast to the priests who remained standing day after day. There were no chairs in the tabernacle or temple.

6. Because of Christ's superior sacrifice, we can have lasting change from the inside out. And because we are changed, we can have a relationship with God unlike ever before.

7. Of course we still sin and feel guilty about it! Anyone who would say otherwise is in denial. As discussed in session 2, we live in an in-between time that theologians like to call the "already-not-yet." Jesus has *already* done the work that allows us to draw near to God — in fact, through Jesus, he views us as perfect! But at the same time, God's kingdom is *not yet* fully here and we still live and sin in a fallen world. And so it will be for believers until Jesus returns a second time (9:28). Until we meet the Lord at our death we are a work in progress and need to continually turn to him for help.

8. Because Jesus is a greater High Priest, and because of his superior sacrifice, we can personally enter into God's presence with full confidence at all times. This is an incredible claim to intimacy with God compared to the

old covenant system. The high priest had to be cleansed, sprinkle blood, and enter the Most Holy Place only at the designated time (the Day of Atonement), language very similar to what we find in Hebrews. However, the common people were not even allowed in the Tent of Meeting during this time. How much more do we have now, actually entering into God's presence after being sprinkled and cleansed by the blood of Jesus.

9. As we gather to worship, we have much to be thankful for:

- We can enter God's presence—made possible only because we are "clothed" in Jesus' holiness thanks to his perfect sacrifice which has removed our sin.
- We can enter into God's presence anywhere, since Jesus links us to the heavenly tabernacle—the earthly one has been done away with.
- We can enter into God's presence anytime, since Jesus' sacrifice was permanent.
- We can stand before God with confidence and joy, not uncertainty and fear, knowing that no more sacrifices are necessary.
- We have an incredible privilege that should express itself in spontaneous and heartfelt worship and joy, which most of us take much too lightly as we enter into "formal" worship.

10. The sooner we admit our need for help and guidance, the stronger we will be. We really need the help of others to encourage us and keep us accountable along the way (see Heb. 10:24). There's no substitute for Scripture reading and prayer to keep us in communication with God, allowing the Holy Spirit to guide and teach us as we grow to greater maturity, better able to withstand the trials and temptations that come our way.

11. If you think of the summary of God's commandments to us—to love God and to love others—it's quite natural to see an exhortation toward love and good deeds in response to being in God's presence. God is not only preparing us as individuals to grow in faith, but preparing us as a community to grow in faith. We won't be on our own in heaven, but part of a bigger community! In response to the improved covenant with God, it is fitting to see an improved covenant among ourselves.

12. Being able to draw near to God is a result of being forgiven and accepted for who we are. As we are loved by God, he encourages us to reflect that love

to those around us. Therefore, encouraging others who might be fearful, anxious, unsure of themselves, etc. should naturally overflow from what we have received from God. On the other hand, it doesn't always come naturally—it's a supernatural phenomenon that comes from a supernatural privilege. Regardless of where you stand now, lean on God to become all the more of an encourager, living and acting in faith because of God's love for you.

# SESSION 6 LEADER'S NOTES

1. Hebrews 5:13 does not just refer to "head knowledge" of God's word, but learning about God's righteousness by having to constantly depend upon it. Of course, understanding how to "think right" is necessary for right actions, but until we actually live by the truths we say we believe, there is no evidence that we really believe and rely on God's righteousness. Such a lifestyle suggests that we have not grown in faithful reliance on God. We learn in the context of community, but we ourselves are the ones who have to put it into practice to learn and grow.

2. As you answer this question, remember the criteria in question 1 — not just head knowledge of God's word, but also evidence of change from applying it to all aspects of your life. Looking back and looking ahead can be useful tools for measuring change.

3. The warning is addressed to those who have been enlightened, tasted the heavenly gift, shared in the Holy Spirit, tasted the goodness of the word of God and the powers of the coming age. There's debate over what these things mean precisely, because no one wants to say that someone who is truly a Christian can completely fall away from faith. But taken at face value, it certainly sounds like the church that's being addressed. As George Guthrie summarizes, "[W]hat this means is that if one comes to the end and does not have a relationship with Christ because of a lack of perseverance, that relationship never was really there in the first place."[1]

4. When Hebrews was written, people *were* in danger of falling away. It was a time when Christians were in danger of persecution and the pressure was great. But churches throughout history always have a mix of people who are truly believers and others who just appear to be — only God can truly tell the difference. It's helpful to remember that this letter is addressed to a corporate audience, not just to an individual who might be floundering. But, as indicated by the previous section, we all go through periods of slow (or even negative) growth. No one should dismiss the warning as not applying to oneself, for the warning reminds us that perseverance to the end is crucial. Anything short of lifelong perseverance puts into question the quality of our walk with God.

5. These and other verses consistently emphasize that God has always warned his people about the consequences of disobedience. Scripture is less clear about the ultimate destination of some who seemed to be part of the family of faith but then failed in disastrous ways. (For instance, will the people who were saved from Egypt but died in the desert be in heaven to greet us? We don't really know.) Perseverance to the end is important! We have to balance such warnings with God's promises to never leave us or forsake us (e.g., 13:5) — both are equally true.

6. They are crucifying the Son of God all over again and subjecting him to public disgrace (6:6). They deliberately keep on sinning despite knowledge of what is required of them (10:26). They show contempt for God's Son, consider his sacrifice insufficient, and insult the Holy Spirit (10:29). These are not people who are merely backsliding for a while; having once identified with the Christian community, they are now deliberately living counter to God's ways and announcing it to the rest of the world in defiance.

7. It's impossible to be brought back to repentance after they have gone that far (6:4–6). If they reject Christ's sacrifice, there's nothing else that can save them (10:26). They should be prepared for terrible judgment — Old Testament judgment by fire is brought to mind (see for instance Lev. 10:1–3). Whatever their judgment looks like, "it is a dreadful thing to fall into the hands of the living God" (Heb. 10:31).

8. The author of Hebrews has seen evidence of their faith worked out in their lives in the past — things that accompany salvation (6:9). They have been instrumental in helping "his people," possibly referring to help in the midst of persecution (further elaborated on in 10:32–34). But God is the one who will be the final judge of their actions and motivations (6:10). They must continue to the end in order to "make their hope sure" (6:11) — not by passing some threshold requirement of good works but by showing evidence of their lasting faith and hope.

9. Diligence, perseverance, not shrinking back, imitating those who have continued to the end — the message here is pretty clear. We've got to keep going in our faith and not slack off. Our salvation is not a one-time event but a continuing process. The fact that he describes them as guilty of being *nostros* and encourages them not to become *nostros* at the same time could mean that he's addressing different people in a corporate audience,

but he could also be addressing the struggle that's in all of us simultaneously — to slack off or keep running the race — which is why the warning is so pertinent.

10. Abraham was called to believe God, act in faith, and then wait patiently for God's promises to be fulfilled. God made an oath — swearing by himself since there is nothing or no one greater — to prove that his promises are true. It was God who provided an alternate sacrifice, to prove himself true to his prior word. This incident also points ahead to a greater fulfillment of his word, when God provides Jesus, his only, his beloved Son, as a sacrifice for all. By such acts, we know that God's word is reliable and trustworthy, and that his purpose is unchanging, so when he makes a promise we can believe him.

11. These verses provide another word picture — that of an anchor in a storm. Because God's promises are trustworthy, it allows us to have perspective and patience to weather the circumstances and remain anchored regardless of the storm. Our hope is not based on our own faithfulness, but on God's, which never fails. "And hope does not put us to shame, because God's love has been poured out into our hearts through the Holy Spirit, who has been given to us" (Rom. 5:5).

12. The author of Hebrews does not mince words regarding the truth since he does not want his audience to slip away from the faith. However, he also encourages us so that we would want to rise to the challenge rather than mope in our failures. The hope he offers through Christ is too good to let go of. We would do well to follow his example.

## NOTE

1. Guthrie, 231. (See Guthrie, 223–232, for a fuller discussion.)

# SESSION 7 LEADER'S NOTES

1. Faith is being sure of what we hope for and certain of what we do not see. The hope expressed here is reflected in the second half of the definition—a certainty, even though we don't see it yet. This is very different from the emotional complacency reflected in statements like, "I hope it doesn't rain and spoil our picnic," or "I hope I'll see you sometime." Biblical hope demonstrates a confidence in the promises of God rather than just wishful thinking. The definition seems to capture the very essence of what faith is about, although there is much that can be said to flesh it out, as evident in the next question.

2. 11:3 points to a fundamental understanding of God as the originator of the universe. It also points to him being something other and greater, going beyond what our finite minds can imagine, regardless of how far science develops in describing the mechanisms of how things in the universe work.

   11:6 builds on 11:3. We must believe God exists in order to have faith in him. Only then can we hope to please him, and in response be blessed by him.

   11:7b establishes that faith is not neutral. Those with faith call into question the beliefs of those without faith, and point to something greater that goes beyond life as we see it.

   11:10 builds on 11:7b, a more concrete conception of "something greater that goes beyond life as we see it." Here the author envisions a perfect and more permanent city, or establishment of God (also reflected in 11:13–16), in contrast to the society and structures we deal with now.

   11:13 expands on 11:10, recognizing that there is something better that we long for, that enables us to release our grip somewhat on what this life offers.

3. Although obvious, we don't want to skip the repetitive phrase "by faith" which characterizes all the examples. More subtly, there seems to be a progression of basic faith in God to a more personal understanding of life with God that goes beyond our present lives. All the examples demonstrate a basic trust, submission to, and identification with God that goes beyond the visible.

4. There are an incredible number of people over time who have been faithful through difficult circumstances, but God has also shown himself to be faithful to his people and his plan through the darkest of times. Knowing this produces both hope and challenge.

5. You could safely say that all the examples of faith listed in the chapter faced opposition, particularly because of their faith, yet they persevered and are remembered for significant steps in building the kingdom of God. This would help the original readers to see the big picture and realize they are not unique in their struggles. Perhaps more importantly, the evidence of God's faithfulness in the past could encourage them to hang tough through their current hardships. They might also see themselves as a critical link to future generations of faithful believers, as the characters in chapter 11 were for them.

6. While it's confusing as to how some names made it onto this list, it's also comforting. None of us "deserves" to be on this list, yet God's grace is all the more evident when we see how he uses ordinary, sinful human beings for his purposes. When we are forgiven because of Christ, God sees us through Christ, and we become heroes of the faith in his eyes; our sinful deeds are truly forgotten from the record.

7. Since the author of Hebrews was focusing on the Old Testament to support his point (and by no means covered everyone possible), there are many examples in the New Testament and in later Christian history of great people of faith. Keep in mind that this does not mean that they were perfect people, but they believed in God's plans even when they couldn't see how those plans could possibly succeed.

8. The "something better" was Jesus, who came to earth, lived a perfect life, and gave himself on the cross in our behalf—all in accordance with God's will. As a result, all of us who have faith—the "hall of faith," the original readers of Hebrews, and current readers—are forgiven and are being "made perfect." In addition, we all started out with the same sinful nature, facing obstacles both from ourselves and from the fallen world around us.

9. Because we are like those who have come before us, struggling with the same sin nature, and facing obstacles just as they did, we should be encouraged to run as they ran—to the end of their lives in faith. We are required

to "throw off everything that hinders and the sin that so easily entangles," and we are to "run with perseverance."

10. Jesus faced hardships and temptations just like the rest of us, yet he persevered faithfully (4:15). In session 4 we looked at how that made him the perfect High Priest. From that perspective he was the perfecter of our faith because his sacrifice was actually effective in forgiving sins. In these verses, Jesus is the supreme example of a faithful person. He was sure of the outcome of God's plan, even though it went against everything that humanly made sense. The shame of the cross was nothing compared to the joy set before him. So he "set the pace" for us in the race of faith as the best anyone could follow, the perfecter of faith, even more than all the examples in chapter 11 put together.

11. None of us voluntarily chooses suffering, but it is part of the package in faith and growth. If the end result were not worth it, it would be easy to give up. But Jesus' confidence in the benefits of an eternal life with God and his victorious endurance in achieving it should help us to take heart and keep going. He sat down at the right hand of the throne of God, and we will follow him across the finish line there—it's a promise (see John 14:1–3).

12. There are obviously things that are part of a sinful lifestyle that need to stop when you take on a life of faith. But beyond that, we struggle with things that are not sinful in and of themselves, that can still keep us distracted from God's goal for us. Consider these things carefully, and do it on a regular basis—they can pop up in different forms again and again throughout life.

# SESSION 8 LEADER'S NOTES

1. The author views hardship as God's discipline, rather than his neglect. It is a sign of being a legitimate and beloved child of God.

2. Only those who have been "cleansed" can walk on the highway called the Way of Holiness. It is for those who are walking in God's Way. In these verses, those with feeble hands and knees are encouraged to persevere because God is coming soon to transform the places of hardship into places of blessing. What we have to do is nothing compared to the transformation and blessing God performs.

3. • We know we are loved and accepted (12:6).
   • Discipline is good, and prepares us to share in God's holiness (12:10).
   • It produces a harvest of righteousness and peace (12:11).

4. Answers will vary, of course, depending on individual experiences. But often the greatest lessons in life will go far beyond the period of time our parents have the greatest influence on us, and God will hold firm even when parents will give in, trying to soften the blows on their children.

5. Hindrances or sins include:

   • the "bitter root" that grows up to cause trouble and defile many (12:15);
   • sexual immorality (12:16, 13:4); and
   • love of created things (food, money, and most anything else) more than the Creator (12:16–17, 13:5).

   To use the terminology of 12:1, these things all distract us from the race marked out for us. If our eyes are fixed on problematic relationships, or if our appetite for other things or people is not satisfied within the means that God says is acceptable, our eyes will not be fixed on Jesus and we will stray from the path.

6. • Make every effort to live in peace with everyone (12:14).
   • Be holy (12:14).
   • Don't miss out on the grace of God (12:15).
   • Love each other (13:1).
   • Practice hospitality (13:2).
   • Be merciful to those who are suffering (13:3).

- Honor marriage (13:4).
- Be content (13:5).

These are all things that are pretty straightforward to understand, but harder to put into practice. It's usually easier to see where and how other people could improve, but take some time to think about your own progress.

7. Harking back to Deuteronomy 31:6, God has said, "Never will I leave you; never will I forsake you." This is great comfort, especially during hard times. God doesn't necessarily save us from trials; as we saw earlier in this session, he uses them to discipline us. But he will never abandon us. Furthermore, the author of Hebrews quotes Psalm 118:6, "The LORD is with me; I will not be afraid. What can human beings do to me?" If God—with all the resources of the universe at his command—is our helper, and if death means going to be with the Lord, there is nothing anyone can do to ultimately destroy us. Christian history attests to the difference this truth makes in Christians' lives. If we do not see a difference in the lives of Christians around us, perhaps we need to examine our own hearts to see how we can begin to make a difference. The book of Hebrews was written for just such a purpose—calling people back to the basics and warning them about fruitless lives.

8. Esau was keener on the short-term fulfillment of his stomach than the eternal value of his birthright (Gen. 25:29–34). We might be tempted to say we would never do such a thing, but it's easy to get caught up in other short-term desires which, in the heat of the moment, seem of highest priority. Fortunately, we have a High Priest who understands temptation completely and who can help us in our time of need (Heb. 4:14–16).

9. We benefit from church leaders teaching the word of God and seeing the application of it in their own lives, which gives us worthy examples to imitate. We also benefit from their oversight, since they desire to give account of our growth and maturity. We help them by respecting and obeying them and praying for them.

10. Like the other hindrances that we looked at (see question 5), anything that causes people to fix their eyes on something other than Jesus can cause them to stumble or stray. The ceremonial foods and sacrifices of the old covenant had become obsolete (8:13). If the original readers were drawn

back to those familiar practices, they were missing out on the grace of Christ's work on the cross. Instead they should fix their eyes on Jesus and offer, in response, the sacrifices of praise and of doing good for others.

11. This is not meant to be a critique on any particular style of worship. We can just go through the motions in *any* style of worship. A sacrifice of praise involves concerted effort and concentration focusing on God and responding to the grace he's given us through Jesus. And do not forget to do good and to share with others (13:16). Some churches focus more on verbal praise, others on the sacrifices of helping others. Both are mentioned here as essential and pleasing to God.

12. Many of the things we studied throughout Hebrews are captured in this short benediction. The *God of peace* is the God who loved us so much that he initiated a covenant, established a people, and sent his Son to restore his relationship with us that had been broken because of sin. *The blood of the eternal covenant* refers to the perfect sacrifice of Jesus which finally and eternally cleanses us of sin so that we can come into the presence of our Holy God. Jesus, the *great Shepherd of the sheep*, is the perfect High Priest, who became one of us, calls us "brothers and sisters," sympathizes with all our weaknesses, yet set the path for us to follow him to heaven itself. He *equips you with everything good for doing his will* through his sacrifice on the cross as well as the example he sets for us as the author and perfecter of our faith. God *works in us what is pleasing to him* as he disciplines his children through hardships to transform us into the people he created us to be. And this is all done *through Jesus Christ, to whom be glory for ever and ever*, the one chosen by God, superior to the angels, to Moses, to the other high priests, to all those who went faithfully before him, and who is truly worthy of our praise.

# The NIV Application Commentary

## Hebrews

*George H. Guthrie*

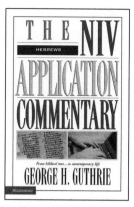

Most Bible commentaries take us on a one-way trip from the twentieth century to the first century. But they leave us there, assuming that we can somehow make the return journey on our own. In other words, they focus on the original meaning of the passage but don't discuss its contemporary application. The information they offer is valuable—but the job is only half done!

The NIV Application Commentary Series helps us with both halves of the interpretive task. This new and unique series shows readers how to bring an ancient message into modern context. It explains not only what the Bible means but also how it can speak powerfully today. The NIV Application Commentary series helps with both halves of Bible study. It builds a bridge from the past to the world we live in—explaining not only what the Bible meant, but also how it can speak powerfully today.

The message of the book of Hebrews can be summed up in a single phrase: "God speaks effectively to us through Jesus." If we can just unpack those seven words of all their theological meaning, we have a way to approach everyone, no matter their age, with the message of the gospel that will demand a hearing.

Printed Hardcover: 978-0-310-49390-7

*Pick up a copy today at your favorite bookstore!*